# Book of Chocolate

*Annie Perrier-Robert*

# Book of Chocolate

Photographs by Frédéric Vasseur

HACHETTE
Illustrated

# Contents

# Introduction

Chocolate has that rare quality of appealing to all tastes, whether it comes as a smooth drink, a refined delicacy or is used as a simple ingredient for making pastries. It plays such an important role that people can't do without it. Its true origins are a mystery. Perhaps that is just as well: fantastic things defy normal categories, mingling history and legend in a mass of confusion, and in the process gaining an almost mythical status.

Today, chocolate is mainly associated with confectionery, far removed from the dietary or even therapeutic benefits that for centuries were linked to it – confectionery not long ago associated with the idea of luxury and celebration and which, formerly the preserve of the well-off, is now much more widely available.

Nowadays, chocolate in bars and boxes, truffles, pastilles and assorted sweets are all part of what we eat regularly. Following the great pioneers of the late 19th century, the industry now has sophisticated and high-powered machines. Alongside them, craftsmen continue the tradition of the 'inventors' of chocolate, forever seeking out new shapes and flavours. Chocolate makers have become magicians by the beginning of the 21st century, playing with all sorts of tastes and aromas, and extracting the 'quintessence' from all the different cocoa beans. Now they can create a confection whose texture is a consistent blend of smoothness and finesse. This is a great art, and in this book we set out to discover its secrets.

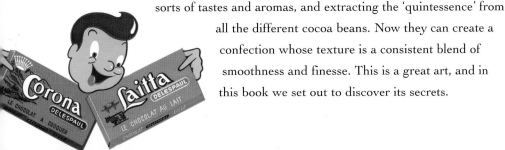

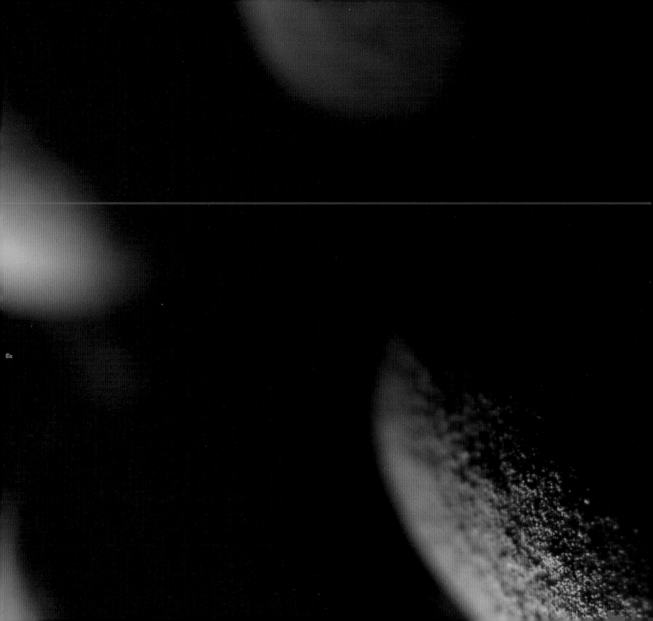

# Chocolate around the world

*Chocolate is a mysterious substance: it was a drink before it became a delicacy, a food before it became a treat. We know for sure that it was 'born' in the tropical forests of Mexico and northern Guatemala, where the pre-Columbian tribes ate the flesh of the fruits of the cacao tree. But its history really began when one of those Indians had the idea of grilling the seeds and eating them.*

# Early legends

*As they advanced from simply gathering a few beans to organised harvests, the Maya were the first to take a real interest in this product of the forest and to develop its cultivation. Alas, we have very little information about this period.*

**Below:**
Engraving from the 16th century showing Indians of pre-Colombian America harvesting cocoa pods.

**Opposite:**
Quetzalcóatl, whose name in the Nahuan language means 'Plumed Serpent' (from *quetzal*, bird, and *cóatl*, serpent). *Codex Telleriano Remensis*, 16th century.

## LEGENDARY ORIGINS

The semi-fabulous beginnings of chocolate took place after the Toltecs had occupied the central Mexican plateau. When Topiltzin, the king of this northern people, ascended to the throne, he took the name of the ancient god of creation, knowledge and culture, Quetzalcóatl, and became his high priest. Around 980, he established his capital in Tula, in the north of the Mexico valley, and made this town into a real hub of civilisation. His mistake was to ally himself with the kindly Quetzalcóatl, to the detriment of the warrior god Tezcatlipoca, revered by the majority of the Toltecs. This bellicose god owed his name, 'Smoking Mirror', to the fact that he observed the actions of men in an obsidian mirror. Angry at being passed over by the king-priest, Texcatlipoca disguised himself as an old man and entered the king's presence, intoxicating him with a strange drink thought to be chocolate and, once he was drunk, made him lose his honour with his own sister, Quetzalpetlatl. His vengeance was complete: in 999, the king abdicated and went into exile.

## A DIVINE TREE

Legend also credits the king-god of the Toltecs, a man famed for his infinite wisdom, with bringing cacao seeds from the sacred lands of the first sons of the Sun, and introducing this tree, created by the gods, into the paradisiacal gardens of the Talzitepec mountains near Tula. Legend also maintains that he trained his disciples to cultivate this tree, and they passed on this knowledge to their descendants, so that the Meso-American peoples could then develop plantations.

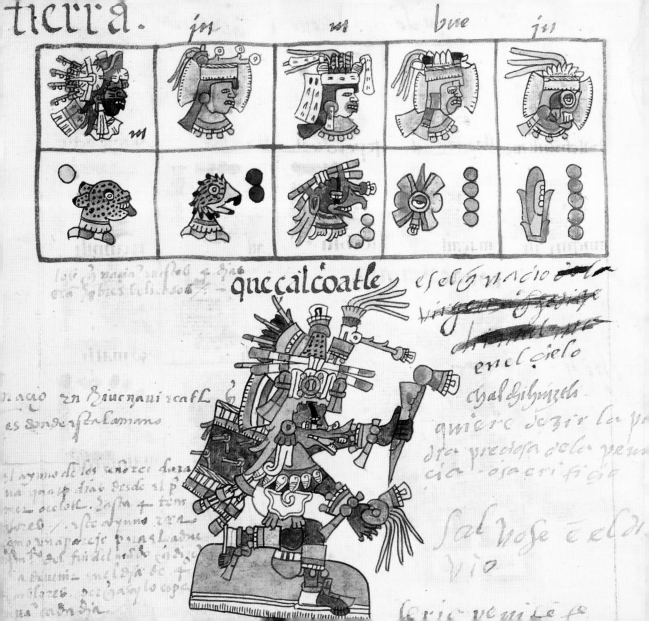

tierra.    jn    m    bue    jn

quecalcoatle            es el figuracio de la
                        virgen ....
                        .......
                        en el cielo
                        chalchihuizteli

nacio en Biueņauircatl y         quiere dezir la pie
es donde esta la mano             dra preciosa dela peni
                                  cia o sacrificio

el ayuno de los señores dura
ua ochenta dias desde el pri
mer ociotl. hasta que tom
...

salio se el dia
vio

...

# The story begins ...

*The real story of chocolate can only be traced from the beginning of the 14th century, when the Aztec empire was formed around its capital, Tenochtitlán, in the area that later became Mexico.*

**Opposite:**
Although Christopher Columbus did not take any notice of the Indians' traditional drink in 1502, Hernán Cortés was quick to see the possibilities. He mentioned it to Emperor Charles V in one of his letters and, on his return to Spain in 1528, brought some beans back with him. During a meeting with the sovereign in Toledo, he encouraged him to taste the exotic drink.

### AN EXCLUSIVE PRODUCT

Cocoa was among the products to be found in market displays. It seems that it was sold ready-prepared, and was beyond the means of many. The Indians consumed a lot of *atolli*, a fairly thick gruel of maize, spiced or sweetened with honey. Chocolate, however, was expensive and only the upper classes could afford it.

Hernán Cortés discovered the drink in 1519, when visiting Moctezuma II. The Aztec king (1466–1520) was famed for the magnifience of his court. In his *True History of the Conquest of New Spain*, completed in 1568, Bernal Diaz del Castillo relates the detailed observations he made when

he was Cortés's companion on the expeditions to Mexico. 'From time to time, he was brought very fine golden cups containing a drink made with cocoa; they said it had aphrodisiac qualities, but at the time we paid no attention to this. I noticed that they served about fifty pots of a drink made from cocoa with lots of froth on it; this is what he

drank, and the women handed it to him with the greatest respect.' After the meal with Moctezuma, the soldiers of the guard were served with more than two thousand pots of the same drink.

## KERNELS USED AS CURRENCY

After the cocoa kernels were dried in the sun, they were kept for a long time, and this is probably why the pre-Colombian peoples chose them as their 'coinage'. They were used for 'transactions in everyday commodities, before the Europeans introduced them to luxury and ambition' (Nicolas de Blégny, 1687). A survey carried out in 1545, after the Conquest, by a Spanish visitor, Gomez de Santillán, gives us an idea of the commercial transactions made there: 20 small tomatoes cost one kernel, a hen's egg was worth 2 kernels, a turkey's egg 3, a Mexican triton (axolotl) 4, a small rabbit 30, a chicken 40, a turkey hen 100, a turkey cock 200, etc. More surprising still, gold was also bought in the same way.

## Chocolate, Indian-style

'There is not a square or market where you don't find a Negress or an Indian woman with her aunt, her apastlet – a vessel like a casserole – and a stick in the form of a spindle [...]. First, these women set aside a piece of chocolate paste or cake, and soak it in water, then they take off the foam, which is the best and principal substance, which they divide among vessels placed round them called Tecometes. Then they serve this to the waiting Indians and Spaniards. They mix in warm Atolli as well, which they keep in pots, and which they think has great qualities and effects. Some want it to be served with a coloured Achiote, a powder or pastille made from a fruit which they say is very effective against colic.'
(Barthelemy Marradón, Spanish doctor from the town of Marchena, 1618)

## On the trail of cacao

According to Fray Bernardino de Sahagun, there was a strange animal in pre-Columbian America, a quadruped larger than an ox. This hacaxolotl, as it was called, was particularly fond of the fruit of the cacao tree. Noticing this, the Indians devised an unusual way of gathering the beans. As Sahagun explained, the animal's droppings 'contained untouched cacao seeds. It left a quantity of them each time. The locals followed its trail and picked up the cacao which it left in this way.'

Once or twice a year, the Indians used these coins to pay their tribute to Moctezuma; hence the vast reserves that the Spanish found in the king's palace.

**A BRISK TRADE**

Throughout the 16th century, cacao kernels and official money worked together in perfect harmony; in 1576, the exchange rate stood at 1120 kernels to 1 Mexican peso. Neither monetary system escaped the efforts of forgers. In a letter to Charles V, in 1537, Antonio de Mendoça reported the following unusual anecdote: 'Fifteen or twenty days ago, someone brought me two false testons [coins] ... I ordered all the goldsmiths in Mexico and the surrounding areas to be arrested, but all our measures failed to discover the truth [...] They have even found a way of counterfeiting the cacao which serves as their coinage, as Your Majesty will see from the samples I am sending.'

Cacao kernels apparently remained valid for quite some time. In the middle of the

17th century, 1,000 kernels were worth twelve and a half reals. At the beginning of the 19th century, 12 to 14 kernels were the equivalent of 1 real. According to Alfred Franklin, they still took the place of billons (ingots) in Mexico in 1850. He added: 'They even had the advantage over metals that they could be eaten once they had been in circulation for long enough.' This is similar to a remark made three centuries earlier by Pedro Martyr de Angleria (*De Orbe Novo*, 1530): 'How fortunate to have money that supplies man with a pleasant food and defends him from the truly infernal plague of avarice!'

## An aid to beauty

**Reports that have been handed down to us about Amerindian civilisations at the time of the Conquest show that women used to coat their faces with cacao oil to give themselves an attractive colour. Ignoring the 'annoying obstructions' which this produced and only seeing its decorative virtues, they ate the cacao beans when the fruit came out, which gave them 'a pale and wan colour, like pale-skinned women who eat earth from pots and wall plaster, like Spanish women often do to give themselves this colour, which they value above all others [...].'**
**(Thomas Gage)**

**Left**:
Drying beans among the Indians. 16th-century engraving.

**Opposite top:**
Engraving taken from the *New and Curious Treatise on Coffee, Tea and Chocolate*, by Philippe Sylvestre Dufour (Lyons, 1685).

# The Spanish conquest

*The Spanish rapidly acquired a taste for chocolate at the end of the 16th century, consuming as much of it as the Creoles and Spanish Americans. It became fashionable among the high society of the day.*

**Below:**
Chocolate was very popular, and often drunk in the street. A *chocolatero* (chocolate seller) in Madrid, by Gustave Doré.

## AN IMMENSE SUCCESS

During the Conquest, the Spanish became intrigued by this mysterious product, surprised mainly by the stimulating and nourishing qualities of the drink made from it. But when they gave cocoa its first name (*amigdala*), they were referring to the use of the kernels as currency by the natives of Meso-America. The drink was widely taken up throughout the Iberian peninsula, becoming an integral part of their diet. And although it was soon possible to eat chocolate in the form of pastilles, as they were made in America under the name of *diablillos*, for a long time people remained reluctant to chew chocolate.

In the 17th and 18th centuries, the drink was consumed at all hours and in all kinds of places. More than a hundred edicts were issued to control its preparation and consumption. In university circles, particularly in Valencia, it became the custom to give the members of the examining board a certain amount of chocolate.

## A WHOLE RITUAL

Chocolate nevertheless remained essentially the drink of the well-off classes. As the Comtesse d'Aulnoy revealed, following a journey in Spain (1679): 'When they get up in the morning, people take iced water, followed by chocolate. [...] At two o'clock in winter, and at four in summer,

CHOCOLAT GUERIN-BOUTRON

[...] they take chocolate and iced waters.'

Chocolate was made in a chocolate pot, and served in an appropriate cup, either tall and narrow with a thick base (*jícara*), or more open with a base that somehow 'fitted into' the plate (*pocillo*). This plate was engraved with a protruding ring to hold the cup, taking its name (*mancerina*) from the Marquis de Mancera who had designed it to avoid chocolate stains getting on the dresses of ladies attending parties. From this noble episode comes the name *marcelina*, used in Spain to describe the chocolate cup and its plate.

Chocolate was first manufactured in Spain, but the government strictly forbade its export, which is why it was not known elsewhere until much later.

# Over hills and valleys

*The introduction of chocolate to Europe took place gradually. The drink became very popular everywhere, and has remained so.*

**Above:**
Gathered round a table, important political figures of the day comment on the qualities of Majani chocolate. This factory was set up in Bologna, at the beginning of the 19th century, by Francesco and Romualdo Majani. It was Giuseppe Majani, Romualdo's son, who achieved the decisive breakthrough. He was not only one of the first to make chocolate in Italy, but a leader in the art of advertising.

## ITALY: THE KINGDOM OF DARK CHOCOLATE

When the Florentine Antonio Carletti returned from a voyage to the West Indies in 1606, he introduced chocolate to his country. For a long time, the Italians only used it as a drink. The *cioccolatieri* mastered the art of making and serving it, hot or cold, and in the 1720s the reputation of the chocolate being served in the cafés of Florence and Venice travelled abroad. The French, Germans and Swiss all became enthusiasts, and the Italians' reputation was assured.

A chocolate industry grew up very early in Italy, in particular in Turin and Milan. Its fame was such that people went there from other countries to serve their apprenticeships.

## IN PRUSSIA, CHOCOLATE IS PRAISED BY GOETHE

In the 1640s, a German scholar, Johann Georg Volckamer, is said to have brought back chocolate to Nuremberg which he had bought on a voyage to Naples. There, too, the drink's therapeutic qualities were its main attraction at first, and it was very successful. Frederick II the Great liked drinking it, particularly with his friend Voltaire. Goethe was also a great enthusiast; it is claimed he always carried a cup with him, and it is true that he praised his favourite drink in his poems.

One of the first factories is attributed to Prince Wilhelm von Schaumberg-Lippe, who built it at Steinhude in 1756. Factories were then set up throughout the country.

### BELGIUM: THE KINGDOM OF PRALINES

Spanish domination in Flanders, and its closeness to France, which was quickly won over to the new drink, helped the spread of chocolate in northern Europe. Although the chocolate-drinking habit was successfully taken up in Belgium, it was not until 1840 that the first chocolate factory appeared, making chocolate 'in the form of bars, pastilles and figurines'; this was the firm of Berwaerts. Many other factories followed in its wake. By the end of the century, Tournai was one of the great chocolate-producing centres.

### A true ritual

Today it is relatively simple to make the powder for preparing drinking chocolate, thanks to the high-powered machinery available. The first powders were perfected by a Dutchman, van Houten. When the cocoa butter is extracted from the paste or liquor, this leaves dry material called 'cake' which, when pulverised, gives cocoa powder. This residue should contain from 8 to 20 parts per 100 of butter according to the classification attributed to the product. The cakes are ground, steamed at 18 to 20°C (64 to 68°F) for one or two days, then pulverised and sieved to provide a dark aromatic powder. Sugar can be added to make *chocolate powder*.

### IN THE NETHERLANDS, AN INVENTION OF GENIUS

The learned treatise of Philippe Sylvestre Dufour, from Lyons, brought awareness of chocolate to the Netherlands in 1685. Four years later, the court of Holland's ruler, William III of Orange-Nassau, tasted it at La Haye. Chocolate was restricted to the wealthy

**Right:**
Advertisement for a chocolate firm in Hanover.

classes for a long time, consumption being subject to heavy taxation from 1699. The country's use of chocolate would have remained insignificant but for the intervention of Coenraad Johannis van Houten, who perfected powdered cocoa in 1828. From then on, Holland occupied an eminent place in the history of chocolate. All the conditions were right for this: the country's location by the sea, which facilitated the import of cocoa beans, the lack of customs levies on imports, and the presence of rivers flowing to the rest of Europe.

### UNDER QUAKER RULE

The English took a long time to adopt chocolate. The drink was long the preserve of the wealthy classes. When its price became more reasonable, the craze for it grew rapidly. Chocolate houses multiplied in London, and remained fashionable until the end of the 19th century. Although the first chocolate factory opened in Bristol in 1728, the growth of English chocolate-making happened mainly in the 19th century, thanks to the Quakers. Two of the world's largest companies still bear the names of the Quaker chocolate merchants, true knights of enterprise, who skilfully built up industrial empires: Cadbury and Rowntree.

**Above:**
A Swiss view of the time England acquired a taste for chocolate – even though individual chocolates were still unknown!

**Below:**
This famous Belgian chocolate firm was created in 1872 by Charles Delacre in Vilvoorde.

# Chocolate in France

*It was Anne of Austria, daughter of Philip III of Spain, who, following her marriage to King Louis XIII in 1615, initiated the court into chocolate drinking. The drink increased in popularity after the marriage of the Spanish Infanta, Maria-Theresa, daughter of Philip IV, to King Louis XIV.*

## A HISTORIC MONOPOLY

Chocolate became such a craze that the time came to make its use official. On 28 May 1659, Louis XIV granted Master David Chaliou, whose premises were located in Paris, the exclusive right, for twenty-nine years (reduced to fifteen years in 1666) 'to make and sell, in all the towns and other places in this kingdom as he may see fit, the said chocolate, whether as a liquor, in pastilles or boxes, or in any other manner he may please, and to that end to order from foreign countries the things necessary for the making of the said chocolate'. The age of chocolate had begun, with the institution of the activity of 'chocolate maker'. When Chaliou's monopoly expired, other merchants set up business in various places.

This image of the *poulain* (foal) with the chocolate bars was created in 1911 by Leonetto Cappiello for Poulain-Orange chocolate, and became the logo of the whole brand. It was reworked by later artists in the following decades, but the silhouette of the animal was always retained.

## A SMOOTH DRINK

The expansion of the market was curiously slow. Although it was much enjoyed by the wealthy and famous, for a long time it was unknown to ordinary people, despite the efforts of Colbert to develop the colonial production of cacao. Was it a drink, a food or a remedy? The controversy raged. Enthusiasts and opponents of the new product confronted each other tirelessly. Otherwise the business expanded, particularly from 1780, when France's West Indian colonies became regular suppliers. Chocolate was slow to become a delicacy. Apart from the bars and tablets that were melted to make the drink, apothecaries and grocers sold it in pastilles and lozenges for medicinal purposes. Not until the beginning of the 20th century did the chocolate industry join the gourmet food trade.

### A GIANT IN BLOIS

In 1825, Victor-Auguste Poulain was born into a family of farmers in Pontlevoy, near Chaumont-sur-Loire in the Loir-et-Cher, and at the age of nine began working as a grocer's apprentice. Attracted to the aura of Paris, he went there very early and, as a shop assistant, learned the art of making chocolate from his boss, a grocer and chocolate

## A taste for mixtures

Among the fashionable chocolates of the 19th century, there were some surprising confections such as Turin chocolate (cacao, sugar, powdered toast or roasted starch, cinnamon), analeptic chocolate made with Persian salep (cacao, sugar, powdered salep), tapioca analeptic chocolate (cacao, sugar, powdered tapioca), sago analeptic chocolate (cacao, sugar, sago), arrowroot chocolate (cacao, sugar, arrowroot), beef chocolate (chocolate, dried and powdered beef), and, stranger still, coffee chocolate (rice, chicory root, white mustard seed, iris root, sweetened milk, olive oil) which is chocolate in name only.

merchant. This gave him the desire, in 1847, to set up on his own as a confectioner. His early years in Blois were certainly difficult, as the competition was severe. But his ambition to make high-quality chocolate was eventually achieved, and from 1858 his business grew in size. The factory he built at La Villette and opened in 1862, the steam-powered factory he started in 1871 and the Société du Chocolat Poulain, which he formed in 1893, were to remain, after his death in 1918, the great landmarks in an exemplary industrial success story.

**Right:**
Chocolate at the dawn of the industrial era. The chocolate manufacturer Lombart, a famous firm at the end of the 19th century, had been founded in Paris in 1760. Its illustrious clients included Madame Victoire and the duchesse d'Angoulême, also known as Madame Royale.

When the slot machine became a toy, moneyboxes delivered tiny bars of Menier chocolate (1950s).

## NOISIEL IN THE AGE OF THE CAPTAINS OF INDUSTRY

Jean-Antoine-Brutus Menier, a manufacturer of pharmaceutical powders, decided to go into making chocolate and in 1825, on a tributary of the Marne, built the hydro-powered factory at Noisiel which became the headquarters of his family 'empire'. The policy of this industrialist, and of his son, Émile-Justin Menier, who took over the business in 1853, was to use the most modern mechanical processes, inaugurate new methods of refrigeration so that chocolate could be made all year round, buy his supplies at source and cut out intermediaries, and so make chocolate a basic food product within reach of the general public. Output continued to grow: from about 700,000 kg (690 tons) in 1854 to some 16 million kg (16,000 tons) by the end of the century!

At the great international exhibitions, the Menier company won many awards for its medicinal chocolate, its chocolate for sore throats and coughs (made with salep, almond milk, tapioca, etc) – popular items in the 19th century! – and its chocolate pastilles. The destiny of chocolate-making owed much to those two men, who managed to impose their innovative genius and ensure that decisive progress was achieved.

## Chocolate according to Massialot (1732)

'Good chocolate is that which is no more than two or three months old, which does not smell mouldy, is not remotely old, or pricked or pierced by little worms, which breed there after a while, mainly when it contains too much sugar. When chewed, it must have nothing repellent to our taste, or reminiscent of spices: for if some spice is dominant, it stings the throat so fiercely that one cannot swallow it with pleasure.'

# Swiss pioneers

*Strangely, Switzerland, the 'land of chocolate' par excellence, only discovered the exotic drink well after Spain and France. This apparently happened in 1697, when Heinrich Escher, the mayor of Zurich, brought some back from a journey to Brussels. For more than a century, chocolate was imported from France and Italy.*

**Right:**
Stamp pictures from a Cailler album (1927).

**Opposite:**
The chocolate industry has Rodolphe Lindt (1855–1909) to thank for the conche process and for inventing fondants (1899).

### A HISTORIC GRINDING MACHINE

The Swiss chocolate industry began at Vevey. Before 1803, there was already a small chocolate factory in the town. But the official birthday is 1819, when François-Louis Cailler (1796–1852) set up a business making and marketing cocoa and chocolate at the place known as En Coppet. In northern Italy he had noted the enormous amount of labour involved in grinding the sugar and the cacao by hand, and he designed a grinder consisting of two stone cylinders turning at the same speed. This machine was the ancestor of the conches. His aim was to produce a chocolate with a finer texture at a more affordable price. He was not immediately able to achieve the latter aim. However, his products were a great success. Talleyrand was one of his customers. The business was carried on by his descendants and grew in size, moving to Broc in the mountain pastures of Gruyère. From 1895 they started making milk chocolate, the invention of Daniel Peter, which became the defining image of Swiss chocolate-making.

### PUTTING MILK INTO CHOCOLATE

It was in Vevey that Daniel Peter (1836–1919), a former candle manufacturer who switched over to chocolate, invented milk chocolate in

1875. After seeing his friend Nestlé adding milk to his flour, he had the idea of putting it with cocoa powder. The results of his efforts brought him almost immediate fame. He himself declared: 'I think I can almost certainly say that nearly all the Swiss manufacturers, if not all, have tried to copy me. This proves the value they place on my creation, and all of them, after fruitless trials, had to give up. At the present time, I do not know of any competitor for my product, except for the milk chocolate cream of the Anglo-Swiss Condensed Milk Company at Cham, a kind of cocoa preserve which does not keep long and certainly does not cater for the same market.' It was an invaluable invention, and one that brought him many fierce competitors.

**Left:**
Jean Tobler (1830–1905) was from Appenzell, and trained as a confectioner in Saint-Gallen and Paris. At first he traded in confectionery specialities made with packaging supplied to him by manufacturers, then he himself became a chocolate maker. With his son he set up the Berne Chocolate Factory, Tobler & Co.

## CHOCOLATES, COCOAS, LUXURIOUS CONFECTIONS

The most famous chocolate firms were started in the 19th century – names known today throughout the world and which we already knew as children! In 1826, Philippe Suchard established his factory at Serrières. In 1830, Charles-Amédée Kohler built his in Lausanne. In 1845, David Sprüngli founded a factory in Zurich, which his son Rodolphe took over. In 1852, Aquilino Maestrani, from Ticino, set up in Lucerne; his success soon made it necessary to move his factory to Saint-Gallen. In 1868, Jean Tobler opened a chocolate factory and confectionery in Berne. In 1879, Rodolphe Lindt started his factory in the same town, and was soon associated with firm of Chocolat Sprüngli.

These companies aimed for high-quality products, and thanks to this and to the inventors already mentioned, the Swiss chocolate industry grew rapidly, soon occupying an important role in the country's economy.

## A famous milk

The chemist and inventor Henri Nestlé (1814–1890) began work in Vevey in 1843. His initial researches were into milk, and the business he set up in 1866 was soon well known for the two main products that he had perfected: baby cereal and condensed milk (1875). This second invention allowed Daniel Peter to industrialise the manufacture of milk chocolate. Nestlé's venture into chocolate was made via the company's relationship with the Peter-Kohler firm, which in 1904 was responsible for making a Nestlé milk chocolate with a smooth flavour, adapted to French tastes, the first in a long line of products. Nestlé's definitive move into chocolate-making came in 1929, when it amalgamated with a group of Swiss manufacturers (Peter, Cailler, Kohler, Chocolats Suisses SA). The group grew steadily in size. Today, Nestlé has become the world's foremost agri-food business.

# Chocolate in advertising

*Attracting the public to chocolate with attractive images… That was the aim of the chocolate firms from the end of the 19th century, as chocolate became more widely available. The poster was a favourite means of advertising, a vehicle made popular by the French artist Jules Chéret. Posters advertising chocolate products were found around the world, reminding people about chocolate as they went about their daily lives and tempting them to buy.*

### A message in pictures

The new possibilities offered by posters attracted many artists, especially in Europe. Some of these were quite eminent figures: great illustrators such as the Czech Art Nouveau printmaker Alphonse Mucha and the French illustrator and poster artist Henry Gerbault. The influence of Art Nouveau was initially apparent, with its taste for ornamentation and its decorative motifs often evoking medieval flourishes. In this manner Eugène Grasset praised the merits of Masson chocolate and Adophe Willette promoted van Houten cocoa.

The Italian Leonetto Cappiello, a very popular poster artist of his time, rejected fashions of the day and brought a new style to the medium, choosing bright colours and depicting movement. The poster he produced for Klaus chocolate in 1903 launched this innovative concept, which at first was accused of being incoherent but was soon taken up by other advertising artists. In 1905 Cappiello also designed the original poster depicting a young foal, which later became the emblem of Poulain.

**Left:**
Leonetto Cappiello's poster for Klaus chocolate, 1903.

## A profusion of posters

All over Europe, especially in France and Belgium, chocolate was praised by many talented hands: Théophile Alexandre (Compagnie Française des Chocolats et des Thés), Henri Gerbault (Charpentier chocolate), Ch Loupot (Cémoi), J Stall (Amieux-Frères), Privat-Livemont (Delacre) and A van Neste (de Beukelaer). In England, Howard Davie extolled Rothwell's milk chocolate in his poster of 1900. Throughout the world, posters were the images of an age, around the beginning of the 20th century, and an aspect of its history: bold pictures of sweet-toothed children, comforting nannies and fiery dark horses that mirrored the wonders of a whole society at this product whose first posters adorned walls and streets everywhere. Manufacturers supplied their distributors with advertising boards made of cardboard, which were then replaced by brightly coloured enamel panels suitable for external use. Products such as Fry's milk chocolate and Rowntree's 'High Class' chocolate were depicted for all to see. In the United States, Waleco advertised their Chocolate Peanut Bar, 'Nina' and their sandwich bar, and posters illustrating Hershey's Sweet Chocolate Milk Kisses were in easy view of the public.

**Left:**
Poster for Cadbury's chocolate, 1906.

# Vices and virtues

*U*ntil the 19th century, chocolate continually aroused fierce arguments about its properties and 'contraindications'. Sometimes praised, sometimes discredited, it was always a subject of the greatest interest to doctors and nutritionists, and its history was more closely bound to its qualities as a food than to its attractions as a delicacy.

# Good and bad effects

*Chocolate was formerly seen just as a drink, and was invested with many virtues. It was a kind of miracle remedy recommended by scientists and doctors to cure a great range of illnesses.*

### IN SEARCH OF TRUTH

Today's medical authorities agree that consumption of chocolate in moderation is to be recommended, as it is for other rich foods. They have also assessed its real benefits. According to Professor Trémolières, chocolate is good for convalescents, for loss of appetite and throat problems (angina, oesophagitis), and also for performing intellectual and physical tasks. Not surprisingly, it is recommended for sporting activities.

### PREJUDICES OVERCOME

For a long time it was thought bad for cholesterol. It has since been demonstrated that the average cholesterol content is 1 mg per 100 g of dark chocolate and 10 mg per 100 g of milk chocolate. This makes its cholesterol supply completely insignificant. Another claim made against it was that it caused bilious attacks and symptoms. It is true that this very deep-rooted prejudice harmed chocolate's reputation for decades. Fortunately, it has been disproved: it turns out that a strong dose of chocolate (50 to 100 g/1¾ to 3½ oz) administered daily to a patient with confirmed liver disease does not affect his state at all, and the hepatic cell bears no trace of it under examination.

All signs seeming to come from a hepatic reaction (hives, migraine, etc) are simply due to an allergic type of food intolerance, such as many other products can trigger.

While it is true that chocolate can cause constipation, like all foods that leave no residue and contain little water, this only occurs after heavy consumption. It is enough to counterbalance this lack by consuming more green vegetables, fruits and liquids.

The energy-giving and stimulating properties of chocolate, its richness in mineral salts and its supply of vitamins make it a very useful food product. This is why it was recommended very early on for feeding children.

# The Cadbury story

*From its humble roots in 1824 Cadbury has become a market leader in chocolate manufacture in Great Britain. Originally a small family business, over a century and a half the company has developed into a highly successful international company and is now one of the world's largest chocolate producers.*

## CHOCOLATE BEGINNINGS

The young Quaker, John Cadbury, first founded a shop in 1824 in Bull Street, Birmingham, trading in coffee and tea. He gradually added cocoa and drinking chocolate to the range, prepared himself using a mortar and pestle. John's Quaker upbringing led him to provide tea, coffee and cocoa as an alternative to alcohol, which was believed to be responsible for deprivation and misery among working people of that time. By 1831 John Cadbury was manufacturing these products, producing them in an old malthouse in Crooked Lane, Birmingham, and this was the start of Cadbury as we know it today. In 1847, the business moved to Bridge Street, which provided larger premises and a canal link to the major ports of Britain, and remained there until 1878, by which time the business had expanded even more. Cadbury set up in its current location of Bournville, where it now occupies one of the largest chocolate factories in the world.

**Above:**
John Cadbury, 1801–1889.

## SOCIAL REFORM

In 1861 John Cadbury had retired, handing over the business to his eldest sons, George and Richard, who shared a

**Above:**
George Cadbury, 1839–1922.

new and exciting vision of the future, determining to break away from the standard Victorian industrial scene with its poor working conditions and housing and, instead, provide a decent working environment within a village community.

As well as successfully developing the business, these two social pioneers helped to transform the life of the working classes in Great Britain. George was a housing reformer and built houses on the Bournville site for his workers, providing affordable housing in pleasant surroundings. In time, to protect the land and the houses from developers, George turned his Bournville building estate into a charitable trust, 'The Bournville Village Trust', a completely separate entity from the Cadbury business. Today there is still a strong link between the Cadbury family and the Trust, which continues to make a positive contribution to the housing needs of the 21st century.

In addition to housing and social reform, the Cadbury brothers were pioneers in introducing educational resources for their employees, as well as industrial relations and employee welfare. Cadbury was the first company to introduce a half-day holiday on Saturdays and to close the factory on Bank Holidays.

### CHOCOLATE EMPIRE

Over time, Cadbury joined forces with an older and smaller chocolate manufacturer, J S Fry & Sons, which they assimilated in 1935 as a wholly owned subsidiary.

Today Cadbury has a wide range of products, of which the two main types are Cadbury Dairy Milk (milk chocolate) and Cadbury Bournville (plain chocolate).

# The food of Venus

PAUL & VIRGINIE

*This description attributed to the Viennese doctor Johann Michael Haider dates from the Age of Enlightenment when, more than ever, chocolate was credited with rare qualities in the field of amorous stimulation.*

### LEGENDS OF THE CONQUEST

The Indians of New Spain saw the cacao tree as the tree of the god Quetzalcóatl, famous for giving fortune and power, including sexual power, and they believed that chocolate aroused desire. According to Bernal Diaz del Castillo, historian of the Conquest, the Aztec emperor Moctezuma II drank chocolate before visiting his harem and honouring his many wives. But we should not forget that at this time they liked to add to this drink a dose of a certain Mexican pepper, said to be exciting.

### DEFENDING MORALS

However that may be, this special reputation travelled to Europe. In the 17th century, it aroused much controversy, particularly in religious circles. In 1624, the theologian Johannes Franciscus Rauch, complaining about the unreasonable use of the drink in monasteries, even demanded it should be totally

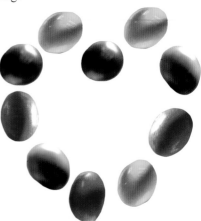

banned in devout places. Without joining the debate, scientists eventually supported the belief in chocolate's aphrodisiac properties.

### FAMOUS CONSUMERS

In the 18th century, the belief was widely held. Casanova, famed for his amorous conquests, was said to prefer chocolate to champagne. The comtesse Du Barry, it was asserted, gave it to her lovers to drink. This idea of chocolate as an incitement to lust was maintained throughout the 19th century, though not so strongly.

### TRUE OR FALSE?

The desire to see chocolate as encouraging amorous behaviour can largely be explained by the presence in cacao of 'psychopharmacological agents'. On the one hand, theobromine, an alkaloid stimulating the nervous system, and, on the other, phenylethylamine, an arousing substance found in the human brain which is linked to the feeling of being in love. Moreover, everyone agrees that some people, prone to affective order problems and suffering from depression, find refuge in eating chocolate. Chocophiles are likely to consume large amounts of chocolate to compensate for a lack of affection. This strengthens the idea that anti-stress properties are present, which distances us from the image of a 'food of Venus' held dear in previous centuries.

CHOCOLAT DE LA C<sup>ie</sup> FRANÇAISE

RUSSIE

## Images of chocolate

*Although not as spectacular as the posters, but full of charm and a certain naïvety, chromolithographs were once very popular. Today, people are more rootless and so more more curious about their past, and find these chromos delightful.*

CHOCOLAT. FÉLIX POTIN

Iris.     Allemagne.

**Above right:**
The famous firm of Félix Potin was inspired by the ambition of a farmer's son from Arpajon. Destined to be a notary, he wanted to become a grocer in Paris and make his own products. He began as a chocolate maker. His boutique in the rue du Rocher and its branch in the boulevard Sébastopol, opened in 1859, grew rapidly during the Second Empire.

**Below right:**
The Chocolaterie d'Aiguebelle, founded in 1869 in the Trappist monastery at Grignan (Drôme), expanded dramatically from 1884. It made full use of chromos in its advertising.

*A new art*
Lithography, a method of 'engraving' on a plane surface, was invented in 1798 by the German Alois Senefelder. Though limited, it soon provided

NOTICE SUR LE MONASTÈRE ET LA CHOCOLATERIE D'AIGUEBELLE

CHATEAUBRIAND

a means of expression for popular imagery. At first it was expensive, as using the stone obviously limited the production of images, but once a steel plate was used instead of the stone, it could print on a larger scale. For some decades, this new kind of 'lithography' was restricted to printing in black or one colour only, and the addition of further colours had to be done by hand. Then the principle of chromolithography was developed in 1837 under Godefroye Engelmann, printing one colour over another in register; the number of plates used depended on the quality of the image desired (sometimes 20 or more).

### A much sought-after advertising medium

Chromolithography became a true artistic technique for advertising. Images abounded, cleverly concealing the artful way the manufacturers tried to enchant the buyer while pushing home their message. At the end of the 19th century and at the beginning of the 20th, the chocolate

firms were all seduced by this means of expression, which could be used in so many ways. Looking through

the chromos which have come down to us, we can see their educational mission. They were meant to instruct people. Often, too, there was a text on the back giving information on the subject being treated.

The famous Swiss chocolate makers Kohler and Klaus also used chromos to entice their customers.

# From the forests of equatorial America to the shores of Africa

*T*he Indians of pre-Columbian times called this miraculous, divine tree of nourishment cucahuaguahuitl or cacaotal. *Later, it was also called a 'cacao tree' or 'cocoa palm'. Then in the 18th century the Swedish naturalist Carl von Linné gave it the learned name of* Theobroma Cacao L, *thus elevating cacao to a 'food of the gods'.*

# A magic tree

*The cacao tree probably came from Central America and the north of South America, where at one time it grew spontaneously in the dense forests of low-lying regions, in a warm and humid climate.*

**Right:**
Engraving taken from Nicolas de Blégny's *Le Bon Usage du Thé, du Café et du Chocolat ...* (1687).

**Opposite:**
Engravings from E Delcher's *A Historical and Chemical Study of Cacao* (1837).

## A FRAGILE TREE

The cacao tree is member of the Malvales, an order of angiosperms that also includes the cotton plant and the large family of the Sterculiaceae.

It grows at an altitude between 200 and 800 m (660 and 2,600 ft) near the Equator, between latitudes 20°N and 20°S. It has certain climatic requirements: a constant temperature of about 24–26°C (75–79°F) and rainfall in excess of 1300 mm (51 in).

It is a fragile tree; it cannot tolerate very strong winds, which uproot it easily, nor temperatures below 15°C (59°F), nor dryness. The nature of the soil is obviously important too. It must be deep, crumbly and rich in organic matter. Alluvial soils suit it perfectly.

## ITS WORST ENEMY

When it is young, the cacao tree is particularly afraid of the sun, which dries out the soil around it. Traditionally

it is protected by planting trees that give it the shade it needs. Banana trees, maniocs, cotton plants, lemon trees and silk cotton trees are its favourite 'protectors'. Also the erythrina or coral tree, which carries dense vegetation and grows rapidly.

In Spain and in America, these trees are called *madres del cacao* ('mothers of the cacao'). When the tree is adult, its foliage can provide dense shade with a diameter of around 6 m (20 ft), enough to prevent the soil from drying out; other shade-providing trees can then be cut down. Today it is thought that the tree produces better when there is no such shade.

### THOUSANDS OF FLOWERS

The tree grows to a height of 10 to 15 m (33 to 50 ft). However, it is cut back regularly so that it measures from 6 to 8 m (20 to 26 ft); this gives it more vigour, stops it spreading too wide and makes it easier to harvest. The trunk is irregular and gnarled, and never exceeds 30 cm (12 in) in diameter. The bark is relatively fine with silvery glints on a brown background, and covers a pinkish wood with a porous texture. Its foliage is dense and continuous; when leaves

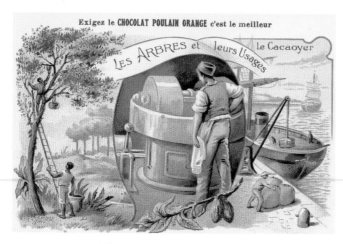

Exigez le **CHOCOLAT POULAIN ORANGE** c'est le meilleur

LES ARBRES et leurs Usages — Le Cacaoyer

Cacaoyer.

fall, new ones are always developing. These are oblong and pointed, 20 to 30 cm (8 to 12 in) long, sometimes slightly dentate, pale green or pale pink according to variety, turning a fine dark green or purplish brown or. Two or three years after planting, the foliage is brightened by a host of tiny white or slightly pink flowers. These scentless blossoms flower in small bunches, even on the trunk and the thicker branches, and last for only about 48 hours. Each tree produces 6,000 flowers at a time, and some 50,000 to 100,000 flowers each year! They are small and have a thick pollen that the wind cannot disperse, which makes pollination difficult. This is further checked by the structure of the flower and the absence of attractive elements (nectar, aroma), and is generally carried out by local midges.

### A MOST UNUSUAL FRUITING PROCESS

Flowering continues almost throughout the year, even during the fruiting period. The fruits are called 'cocoa pods', and are joined to the trunk and branches by a short peduncle. The number of fruits has no relation to the number of flowers: out of some 500 flowers, only one will bear fruit. The majority of the fruits fail to ripen. The large pods ripen in four to five months, their shells changing from green to yellow or orangey red; when ripe, they give off a dull sound when lightly tapped.

## THE PRECIOUS BEAN

Cocoa pods are 15 to 25 cm (6 to 10 in) long and 7 to 9 cm (3 to 3½ in) wide; the pod weighs 400 to 600 g (14 to 21 oz) when ripe. Their thick shells, covered with tubercules, are marked by fairly pronounced furrows running lengthways. Inside, 30 to 40 seeds (beans), with purple skins, are divided into five rows in the middle of a whitish, fairly thick and acid-tasting mucilaginous pulp. Formerly known as 'Mexican beans', the flattened oval seeds are 2 to 2.5 cm (¾ to 1 in) long. They consist of a seed – itself formed from 2 furrowed cotyledons holding a 'germ' (embryo) – and the shell which covers them, brown and brittle on the outside and with a fine whitish layer inside. Eaten raw, the bean gives little nourishment and is difficult to digest. The taste is bitter and astringent. On the other hand, when roasted, it becomes highly nutritious, and it is on this that chocolate is based.

LA GUINÉE-FRANÇAISE

CACAO

FEMME de la GUINÉE

## Facts & figures

- The tree matures at 12 years old and reaches its best production capacity at about 25 years old.
- It generally lives no more than 30 or 40 years.
- 20 to 90% of the young fruits dry up before reaching maturity.
- The average weight of the beans per pod is between 100 and 200 g (3½–7 oz).
- The average weight of the shelled bean is 1.3 to 2.3 g (a tiny fraction of an inch).
- A good tree produces 20 to 25 pods a year, which provides 1 to 2 kg (2 to 4½ lb) of dry beans.
- A cacao plantation does not begin to make a profit until after about 6 years.
- A profitable plantation must produce 1 to 1.5 tonnes per year of dried beans per hectare.

**Opposite below:**
Cacao tree, from an engraving of 1867.

# Types of cacao tree

*Very soon, the various cacao trees will all be officially classified. But these classifications should not ignore the more precise method of differentiation that was drawn up in the 19th century and developed in the 20th century, as people's knowledge increased about the tree and how it grows.*

### DISAPPEARING VARIETIES

The most renowned variety is the *criollo*, an indigenous variety whose oldest plantations go back to the 17th century. It is mainly found in America (Venezuela, Colombia, Mexico, Ecuador, Nicaragua, Guatemala), but also in some parts of Asia, particularly in Sri Lanka. However, the species is fragile, with poor resistance and prone to disease; its yield is small, amounting to only 10% of global production. The pod is elongated and green, or even orangey, before turning red on maturity; it has a warty but fine and tender bark, hollowed with deep furrows. The beans are almost round and full, and vary in number; the cotyledons are almost white. This variety produces very aromatic cocoas with a smooth and slightly bitter flavour, which are used for making 'superior' chocolate or are blended with African cocoas.

### A MORE RESISTANT TYPE

Unlike the criollo, the second species, called *forastero* ('foreigner'), is more vigorous and also extremely productive. It is found over a wide geographical area. Originally from South America, particularly Brazil, it also grows in Java and Sri Lanka; but the region it does best in is West Africa. It produces 70% of the world's total. The pod is generally

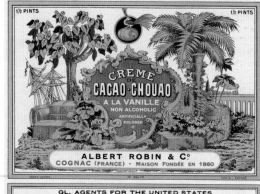

CRÈME DE CACAO-CHOUAO
A LA VANILLE
NON ALCOHOLIC
ARTIFICIALLY COLORED

½ PINTS · ½ PINTS

ALBERT ROBIN & C°
COGNAC (FRANCE) - MAISON FONDÉE EN 1860

GL. AGENTS FOR THE UNITED STATES
ERNEST BLOCH & C° - 100, FIFTH AVENUE - NEW-YORK

almost round and yellow when mature; it has a smooth, thick and hard bark, with shallow furrows. The beans are fairly flat in shape and always the same in number; the cotyledons are dark crimson.

The 'standard' cocoas produced by by the forastero have a light aroma and a strongly bitter taste; they are used to make everyday chocolate.

### SINCE THE 1970S: HYBRID TYPES

The *trinitario* is a hybrid obtained in the 18th century with criollos from Trinidad and forasteros from the Upper Amazon. Today it accounts for 20% of global production. At first it was cultivated where the criollos grew, but is now tending to replace the forasteros. It is found in South America, the West Indies, Africa, Asia, and even in Oceania. The pod is elongated, red or yellow when mature, and marked with about ten deep furrows; its bark is warty and fairly thin. The beans are almost round and contain white or purple cotyledons. The yield is high but the quality is rather variable.

**Left:**
In *Le Bon Usage du Thé, du Café et du Chocolat ...* (1687), Nicolas de Blégny describes the varieties in existence in his day: the large black (A), the largest and best variety, with a blackish brown shell; the small black (B), the same colour but sometimes having more flavour than the large black; the large red (C), with a brownish red shell and a less pleasant taste.

**Below:**
A plantation in the old days.

# Characteristic flavours

**EACH CACAO HAS ITS OWN QUALITIES**
American plantations continue to supply the finest cacaos. Those from Brazil are rich in cocoa butter. Those from the West Indies, Trinidad in particular, are very aromatic. Those from Ecuador are the most sought after, and those from Venezuela are considered to be the finest of all.

But all these South American cacaos, with their incomparably subtle aromas, are very fruity and too robust to be used in a pure state. When blended with African cacaos to make high-quality chocolate, they generally contribute 10 to 25% of the blend. African cacaos are less aromatic, but their quality is improving all the time. Asiatic cacaos are 30 to 50% cheaper than African types, but lower in quality in terms of traditional chocolate-making. Industrial manufacturing methods nevertheless manage to correct their bitterness. They are more suitable for making milk chocolate and coating chocolate.

**FINE CACAO**

The denomination 'fine cacao' ('fine' or 'flavour'), regulated by the International Agreement of 1980 on Cacao, approved by the law of 30 June 1982, only applies to specific cacaos produced in certain countries. It totals less than 8% of global production and its prices are consequently very high.

## Evocative names

The different varieties of cacao have been allotted commercial names corresponding to the embarcation ports most often used for shipping the beans: Bahia and Para in Brazil; Maracaïbo and Puerto Caballo in Venezuela; Guyaquil in Ecuador, etc. The name may also reflect the producing country, for example Trinity, Grenada, Martinique, Guadeloupe, Haïti, Ivory Coast, Ghana, Fernando Po and Nigeria.

# Harvest time

## TWO HARVESTS

The main harvest extends from September to December in West Africa and Brazil, and takes place from April to July in Ecuador; the pods are a good size and the beans very fine. The other harvest takes place from March to May in West Africa and Brazil, and from August to December in Ecuador; the pods are fewer in number and smaller, and the beans less fine. In the West Indies, Venezuela and the island of Trinity, there is just one harvest, from January to April.

The pods are cut from the tree with a knife or machete, and opened as soon as possible, at the latest four days after picking. The pod is traditionally split with a machete or club, taking care not to damage the beans. More and more, though, machines are taking over from men.

## THE BIRTH OF COCOA

In the twenty-four hours following the opening of the pods, the beans are extracted from the pulp, placed in wooden crates whose bases are pierced with holes (fermentors) and covered with banana leaves or old sacks. They are left like that for three to ten days, depending on the variety and the quality desired, and regularly turned. The aim of fermentation is to kill the bean by devitalising the embryo to prevent it from germinating – under the influence of the heat given off and

the acetic acid produced – also to get rid of the pulp, swell up the cotyledons and then, by modifying the chemical components of the bean through hydrolysis, to give it its characteristic brown colour, to reduce its bitterness and the astringence of the taste, finally giving shape to the 'pre-aromas' of the cocoa.

After fermentation, it is advisable to reduce the level of humidity to 8%, even to 6.5 or 6%. Drying is carried out in raised racks, exposed to the sun but sheltered from rain and nocturnal humidity. Drying can also be done on the ground or on expanses of concrete. The beans are spread out in even layers no more than 3 to 4 cm (1 to 1½ in) thick. In the course of this operation, they have to be moved regularly to activate the drying process.

**Opposite:**
Indian extracing beans from the *mazorcas* (pods); 19th century engraving.

**Below:**
Opening the pods is still usually done by hand, needing a large labour force.

LE CACAO

# The producing countries

*The problems of growing cacao trees have been completely mastered. However, the cultivation process varies from country to country.*

**Opposite:**
Many small animals love the mucilaginous pulp covering the cocoa beans inside the pod. Monkeys, squirrels, rats and other rodents are always on the lookout for beans.

### THE SAGA OF THE 'COLONELS OF CACAO'

Production in America fell remarkably during the 20th century. Nevertheless, Brazil, followed by Ecuador, is still one of the world's major producers. The plantations grew up in the Ilheus region, in the south of the State of Bahia, which today provides 95% of Brazil's production. The attraction that cacao exerted there for a long time, as an apparent source of both riches and power, was not unlike a gold rush. The works of Jorge Amado offer the best description of how this hostile land of virgin forest was cleared and 'civilised' with cacao plantations. The Brazilian writer was born on a plantation in 1912, and his childhood was dominated by cacao. His parents were ruined in 1914 after a flood, but managed to build up enough savings to 'start attacking the uncultivated forest once more, opening up roads and planting acres of cacao'. Their new settlement was a growing hamlet which eventually became the town of Itajuipe. 'It already consisted of a long street with houses mixed in among the warehouses for storing cacao.' Adventurers flocked there, searching for 'the richness of the world', 'people without faith or law, rebels of every kind'. Following *Cacao* (1932), the novel which brought the writer great popularity in Brazil, his *Child of Cacao (O Menino grapiuna)* used the author's childhood memories

CHOCOLAT POULAIN — GOUTEZ ET COMPAREZ ! QUALITÉ SANS RIVALE

NICARAGUA

## Refreshing ...

Before it was rejected in favour of the beans, the sugary taste of the pulp inside the pod was much enjoyed by the Indians of pre-Columbian America. In cacao-producing countries in the 19th century, the pulp-eating habit was still practised. In 1834, the *Magasin Pittoresque* showed how the pulp was used after fermentation: 'The winey liquor remaining in the vat is pleasant to drink, and rum can be distilled from it.' At the end of the century, *Le Journal des Confiseurs* provided another recipe: 'People make good use of the gelatinous and fondant pink pulp covering the cacao beans, whose pleasant acidity makes for a popular refreshment [...]. This pulp is prepared with a little sugar and orange flower water, and is a delicacy among Creole women.'

to build a portrait that was both poetic and pitiless about the region, where only the lure of easy money justified becoming a *grapiuna*, as the people of cacao country were known. Nature was hostile, full of venomous snakes and infested with disease, a place where smallpox, malaria, malignant fever and other epidemics decimated populations. It was a world of violence, where the rich landowners, known as 'colonels' from the colonel's trading licences they had acquired in the 19th century, were constantly at the mercy of armed bands.

### THE DAZZLING RISE OF AFRICA

Although in 1895 Africa only exported 7% of the world's cacao production, by 1960 this had reached 72% and put it in the front rank of producers. Since then, it has constantly retained its share. The Ivory Coast has become the world's foremost producer, far ahead of any other country. There the industry involves a great number of small farmers, for whom the beans are vital resource – and this in a country where they do not consume cocoa products, unlike the other producing countries. At present they export cacao in the form of beans (80%) and butter, paste and cake (20%). In addition to the Ivory Coast, other West African countries are involved, such as Ghana, the world's second largest producer, Nigeria and Cameroon.

## COMPETITION FROM ASIA

In Africa, the plantations are still family concerns – from
2 to 10 ha (5 to 25 acres) – while in Asia, as in Latin America,
they are vast estates managed in an industrial manner.
The Asian countries' penetration of the cacao market is one
of the remarkable events of the late 20th century.
From around 1985, it took Malaysia just a few years to rank
among the world's main producers. The
plantations are concentrated in the Malay
peninsula (Western Malaysia) and in the
State of Sabah, formerly British North
Borneo, in the north of the island of
Borneo (Eastern Malaysia), and went
from 10,000 ha (25,000 acres) in 1975
to some 450,000 ha (1,111,500 acres)
in 1989. But in the middle of the 1990s,
its production was reduced by half, and,
taking advantage of an equally spectacular
result, Indonesia overtook Malaysia to
become the world's third largest producer.

**Below:**
The plantation of Valle-Menier,
between Nandaime and Rivas in
Nicaragua, from a 19th century
engraving. In 1862, Menier
acquired this 1,500 ha (3,700 acre)
property in Central America to supply
its European factories with beans.

# Cocoa beans, the raw material

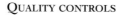

*The checks and controls carried out before the beans are exported, and during the marketing process, help to enhance the quality of the finished products.*

### QUALITY CONTROLS

The many abuses practised by certain cacao producers led to the setting up of rigorous criteria that planters are now obliged to follow when they market their produce. Cacao is one of the raw materials known as 'extrovert', meaning that nearly all the production is exported, and since its production is limited to a small number of countries, the State plays an increasingly important role in checking its export and import.

Standards, established by various bodies both national and international, have been agreed to guarantee the quality of exported beans. The beans are compulsorily subjected to fermentation and must be properly dry, their humidity level not exceeding 7.5%. They must not bear any mark of change (mould, for example) and must be free of all foreign bodies. In addition, they must not emit any abnormal smell, as from mould, smoke or insecticide.

To complete its specifications, the Food and Agricultural Organisation has established a classification of batches according to the percentage of beans that are mouldy, slate-coloured (not fermented) and defective (flat, moth-eaten or sprouting). Several producing countries support these measures.

## Another quality system

The classification in force in the cacao business, recognised by the main commercial asociations, divides the beans into the following categories:

• *good fermented*, which must not contain more than 5% of slate-coloured or 5% of defective beans.

• *fair fermented*, which must not contain more than 10% of slate-coloured or 10% of defective beans.

• *fair average quality*, which must not contain more than 12% of slate-coloured or 12% of defective beans.

Thanks to these quality requirements, chocolate manufacturers are no longer confronted with the problems of former times, which made the treatment of the beans more difficult than it is today: problems of humidity, which affected the roasting process, and beans of unequal size, which involved highly complex adjustments to machinery and caused a lot of waste.

## The age of snack foods

*A*t the end of the Second World War, the peacetime world found its way of life bound to an industrial civilisation. This encouraged a tendency towards excessive or poorly balanced consumption, which some people called 'bad eating'.

### Chocolate bars for energy

Meals became less formal and the amount of 'snacking' increased as the pace of life speeded up, growing out of control under the impact of mass advertising. In this context, which affected the developed countries led by the United States, the chocolate industry was eager to diversify and set about creating new products that combined a pleasant taste with nourishment and a supply of energy; these became part of the daily diet. This is where bars of chocolate came in, launched on the confectionery market in the 1950s with finely targeted advertising campaigns.

WANTED: HUGE LION TAMERS.

BITE IT. CRUNCH IT. CHEW IT.

### Snack foods

These new products had a dazzling success, notably led by the bars made by the Mars company. At first they were very nourishing, then the low-fat content was increased in recent decades, relying more and more on people's weakness for sweet foods, though not forgetting their role as a filling snack. For forty years Mars used the famous slogan: 'A Mars a day / Helps you work, rest and play.'

**Have a break...
have a Kit Kat**

These bars have a thick chocolate coating, usually milk chocolate, over a fairly smooth, aerated paste rather like nougat with a layer of caramel. Almonds, nuts, coconuts, cocoa, etc give them their specific flavour. Their weight varies between 20 and 60 g (¾ to 2 oz), but their shape never changes, so they can be recognised immediately. Alongside them, from 1978, came bars with a biscuit or wafer filling, then in 1984, cereal bars inspired by 'health foods'.

### Food or delicacy?

Today this family of foods occupies a leading place (55%) in the field of chocolate confectionery sold by the piece. The greatest consumers are Great Britain, the United States, the Netherlands and Australia, and the two main producers are the two multinationals, Mars and Rowntree MacIntosh. Theirs is a world far away from that of real, pure chocolate made according to precise standards; far away too from true gourmandise, being devoid of all nutritional value.

# Chocolate in modern times

*The process of making chocolate is mysterious and alchemical. Since its introduction into Europe, it has never stopped evolving and only really established itself in the second half of the 20th century. The texture and aroma of chocolate depend on rigorous preparation, its taste and quality on the choice of ingredients used. The slightest flaw is evident on tasting. Failure cannot be forgiven, for chocolate, with its halo of prestige, does not tolerate mediocrity.*

# Processing the bean

*The beans are loaded in jute sacks or ventilated containers on board ships sailing from Ghana, Nigeria, Brazil, Venezuela, Ecuador, etc, to land in the receiving ports, ready to be made into chocolate.*

**Below:**
Chocolate production in the 17th century, engraving by Nicolas de Blégny. The grilled and hulled beans were crushed to a paste with an iron roller on a flat stone, heated by a brasier placed underneath.

**Right:**
The liquified cocoa is placed in the press in a cloth sack between two sheets of iron and paper.

## THE TRANSFORMATION BEGINS

When the cocoa beans reach the manufacturer, sieves, brushes, 'cyclones' and magnetic separators winnow, clean and use draughts of air to rid them of all the foreign bodies and impurities picked up after the harvest and during the voyage. When they emerge from the various machines, they are sorted to eliminate those lacking the required maturity or revealing defects. Following this double selection process, the healthy beans are put in silos.

## ROASTING THE BEANS

Chocolate owes its colour, aroma and flavour to the roasting process. Carried out in a rotating metal cylinder, its purpose is to destroy any mould, eliminate part of the acetic acid and reduce the water content, which falls to 2.5% for the cotyledon and 4% for the shell. The constantly maintained heat penetrates the bean without burning the shell. Roasting varies in temperature (from 100 to 140°C/212 to 284°F) and time (between 20 and 30 min) according to the nature of the beans. Superior quality beans are roasted at a lower temperature than ordinary beans.

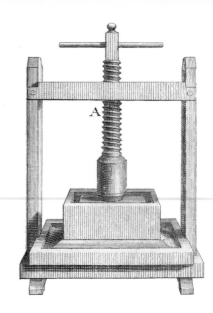

**Left:**
Publicity illustration of the Moreuil chocolate factory, built at Clichy in 1825, showing the roasted cocoa beans being cleaned to get rid of the shells and the seed they contain after crushing.

The size of the beans is taken into account, as well as their maturity, level of humidity and the way they have been dried. The roasting operation also varies according to the product to be made. Today's machines can be programmed to meet all these requirements. They have ventilators which, after roasting, cool the beans as quickly as possible. This sharp cooling process keeps in the cocoa's aromas and prevents fatty matter from getting into the shell.

### THE SECOND STAGE

Roasting makes the shell brittle, making it easier for the beans to be crushed. The shells are cracked between two grooved rollers, then the shells and cotyledons are sieved before being separated by a pneumatic suction process that removes the shell fragments, which are lighter than the cotyledons. In this way, any remaining

**Below:**
Roasting the cocoa in a *Sirocco* roaster, a very advanced machine of its time.

peel or impurities are
eliminated, so that only
the cotyledons remain
(82%). Each of these
contains a woody, non-edible
seed; this is removed using
a de-seeder, into which the
hulled beans are fed. After these cleaning operations, and the
roasting and crushing, the cocoa
beans are some 20% lighter in
weight.

### Nothing is lost

Fragments of shell and peel, still
containing a residue of cocoa
butter, were gathered up and used
in the chemical industry. They
were also used as agricultural
fertiliser, cattle feed, and
sometimes as a fuel. Pharmacies
also used them for the theobromine they contained.

Cocoa butter was used not only
for chocolate-making and confectionery, but also in perfumery
for the preparation of lipstick,
and by pharmacies to make
suppositories.

### THE METAMORPHOSES

The crushed cotyledons (*nibs*)
are hot-ground (50 to 70°C/
122 to 158°F) in cocoa mills.
Since the fusion point of cocoa
butter is at 34 to 35°C (93 to 95°F),
the crushing produces fluid dark-
brown paste known as 'cocoa
paste' or 'chocolate liquor'.
This is chocolate's principal
ingredient. It is cooled and
packed away if it is not to
be used immediately.

CACAO BLOOKER.

Fritz Schön

The roasting temperature is higher for cocoa powder than chocolate. It is reduced when the purpose is to extract cocoa butter to make milk chocolate, which requires a very smooth-tasting butter.

Cocoa butter is essential to chocolate. This fatty matter is extracted from the cocoa paste or nibs at the previous stage. This can be done by a number of processes: pressure, torsion or using a solvent. The standard method is with hydraulic presses, and for industrial chocolate-making, the chocolate paste is submitted to pressures up to 80 t/dm² (750 tons per sq ft). The butter released has a strong aroma. It is filtered to eliminate fibres and impurities, then kept for a time at its fusion temperature so that its crystals can crystallise in their most stable form, then refined to neutralise the acidity and remove its colour and aroma. When it is a clear pale yellow, it can be cooled again and moulded into cakes. Cocoa butter contains about 54–56% cacao from which 42–44% is extracted. It has an essential role in chocolate-making, allowing its products to be kept for a remarkably long time.

## A cocoa infusion

In his *Lessons on Primary Organic Materials* (1881), Georges Pennetier explained that 'the crushed shells are often sold under the name of "cocoa teas": they were used in Ireland and Italy to make a drink known in the latter country as a *miserabile*. By mashing the shells and evaporation of the steam, M Chevalier obtained 26% of a pleasant-tasting extract which, according to him, could be mixed with whole milk to make a drink to rival coffee and tea.'

The scientific author is referring to a preparation almost identical to the one mentioned earlier by Alexandre Dumas in his dictionary of cooking: 'The cocoa beans are lightly roasted; after cooling, the beans are crushed to remove the shells or barks, which are rejected. In Switzerland and Germany, however, they keep them to make an infusion in boiling water which people mix with milk and drink in place of real chocolate.'

# The ingredients of chocolate

*Chocolate-making really begins with cocoa paste and cocoa butter. Other ingredients are then added to these primary materials.*

### A MIRACULOUS 'SWEET CANE'

Texts dating from the time of the Spanish Conquest, or slightly later, mention sugar being used to make chocolate. But this ingredient was not added to cocoa until the Spanish started modifying the way the drink was made.

Initially, sugar was added to the chocolate-making process 'to balance the natural bitterness contained in most of the other ingredients used: and also to help it keep longer, as one does with preserves, which does not prevent it, as it ages, from filling up with little worms, which pierce it like an old cheese, particularly if it is kept in damp conditions or has too much sugar in it' (P S Dufour, 1685). It had a double function, then, the second of which is no longer needed today. However, sugar is still part of the taste of chocolate, and its use is strictly regulated.

### AUTHORISED ADDITIVES

Aromatic substances such as vanilla and cinnamon may also be added to complete some products. Also, to help in the final stages of manufacture, official regulations allow the addition of very small amounts of emulsifiers. These are lecithin from plants and phosphatides of ammonium. The former must be technically pure and no more than 0.2% may be added. The latter may not exceed 5 g/kg, except in the case of

VANILLIER
VANILLENPFLANZE

KOHLER CHOCOLATS FINS

**Below:** At one time, when the sugar arrived at the chocolate factory it was steamed and pulverised to make it blend perfectly with the chocolate.

**Opposite:** Mixers used in former times and those used today demonstrate the passage from hand manufacture to mass production in the heroic age of chocolate-making.

cocoa powder, everyday milk chocolate and chocolate in granules or flakes, for which it can go up to 10 g/kg. Use of these additives is not systematic.

Some edible materials, such as dried fruits, are often involved in chocolate-making. They may be used in a proportion of 5 to 40% of the weight of the finished product if they are incorporated in visible and separate pieces, but must not exceed 30% if they are added in a virtually undetectable form. This addition must be indicated in the description of some finished products.

The whole mixture is blended to obtain a fluid fatty mass with a fine texture, the grinding cylinders continuing until the grains are no more than 20 to 22 microns. Chocolate's smoothness comes partly from this process, and its quality too, provided the work is carried out properly.

FABRICATION DU CHOCOLAT. SALLE DES MÉLANGEURS.

## CONCHING

Conching comes next and turns the chocolate into a stable product. It now takes on its final smooth, bright texture. In addition, the chocolate loses any acridity it may have retained and develops its true flavour. Conching is a dry-mixing process whose purpose is to make the paste more malleable, reduce its humidity level and eliminate any remaining acidity.

At the end of the conching process, the addition of cocoa butter and perhaps of lecithin gives the chocolate its necessary fluidity. All this is carried out in a kneading machine (conch), which at one time was shell-shaped but today is either on a longitudinal axis with granite rollers crushing the paste in a continuous backwards and forwards motion, or, more often, is a circular tub fitted with paddle wheels. The heating and ventilation needed for this process require precise control. Heating is progressive, but must not exceed 80 to 85°C (175 to 185°F) for dark chocolate and 55 to 60°C (130 to 140°F) for milk chocolate. The paste is mixed and rolled in this way for two to three days.

## Sugar: a vital ingredient

For dark chocolate, finely ground granulated sugar is used. For milk chocolate, sugar is mixed with milk; the latter must be whole and in powdered form (sometimes condensed) with 24–25% fat, so that no water can get into the chocolate.

Legislation allows for the use of sugars other than sucrose. As officially defined, chocolate products may in fact contain:

– crystallised glucose (dextrose), fructose, lactose and malt sugar up to 5% of the total weight of the product; this does not have to be declared.

– crystallised glucose (dextrose) in a proportion of more than 5% and not more than 20% of the total weight of the product. In this case, the product description must include the mention 'with crystallised glucose' or 'with dextrose'.

# Temperature controls

*Before the chocolate can be worked (whether dark or milk), the chocolate maker has to get everything at the right temperature. This complex operation gives the chocolate a shiny look, more resistance to breakage and heat, and also guarantees the quality of the moulding.*

## A PRECISE PHENOMENON

In the makeup of chocolate, cocoa butter has a polymorphous nature, solidifying into different crystalline structures in the temperature range 17–35°C (62–95°F). However, the ideal temperature for chocolate intended for moulding or coating is between 24 and 28°C (75 and 82°F), according to the paste. So the task is to avoid producing a diversity of crystals in the cocoa butter.

Temperature controls now gradually cool the chocolate paste, while it continues to be mixed, so as to generate crystals of cocoa butter and integrate them with the mass, which is then reheated to give it the fluidity needed for moulding.

## ADJUSTING FOR TYPE

For dark chocolate, the cooling curve goes from 50–55°C (122–131°F) to 26–28°C (78–82°F), for milk chocolate from 45–50°C (113–122°F) to 25–27°C (77–81°F) and for white chocolate from 40°C (104°F) to 24–26°C (74–78°F). It also varies according to the intended use of the chocolate (moulding, coating, etc). Reheating brings the mass back to 31–33°C (88–91°F) for dark chocolate, 28–30°C (82–86°F) for milk cocolate and 27–29°C (77–84°F) for white chocolate.

This cycle of cooling and heating is carried out in a temperer, a vat with a double boiler. The water temperature and the cooling curve are controlled by means of a thermometer, or a thermostat for automatic temperatures.

# White chocolate

Purists refuse to accept it as true chocolate because it is not made from cocoa paste but is a mixture of cocoa butter, sugar and milk. However, countries such as Switzerland and Belgium make a considerable amount of it. In France, it was not admitted to the ranks of cocoa products and chocolate until the decree of 13 July 1976. Officially, white chocolate is 'a product free of coloring materials, obtained from cocoa butter and sucrose, and from milk or subtances derived from the whole or partial dehydration of whole milk or partly or fully skimmed milk and possibly from cream, partly or fully dehydrated cream, and from butter or butyric fat.'

**Opposite:**
Consistency of the mixture is checked using a spatula on a marble surface.

# The universal bar

*They are the symbol of the enjoyable break and, most of all, of the snack. They are usually made on an industrial basis rather than by craftsmen, on modern machines which make production easier and faster.*

**MOULDS FOR EVERY TASTE**

The liquid chocolate paste is now ready for moulding. The mixture is poured into moulds by means of a weigher, or measuring device, which guarantees the bars all weigh the same. The moulds then pass over a mechanical belt which vibrates continuously so the liquid settles and takes on the shape of the mould, while at the same time getting rid of any remaining air bubbles. The moulds then go into a cooling tunnel, kept at around 6–7°C (43–45°F). The chocolate is cooled and, as it solidifies,

**Right:**
Making chocolate bars in former times. After grinding, the chocolate was poured into mixers, then put through the rover and passed to the weigher, then tapped into place in the moulds.

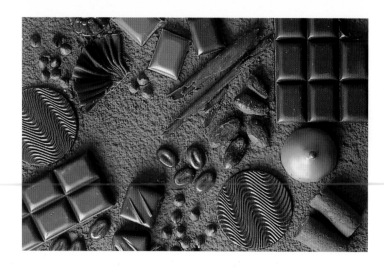

it shrinks in the moulds. It then only remains to remove the bars from the moulds, in a place kept at 14–15°C (57–59°F), and package them. For bars containing a garnish (dried fruit, either whole or chopped), the garnish is added before the moulds are filled and then the same process is followed.

### A MORE DIFFICULT OPERATION

For bars with fillings, the moulds are deeper. Once they are filled, they are immediately turned over so that part of the chocolate runs off and the thin layer adhering to the walls can be solidified in a cooling tunnel. They are turned over again, then the

'Standing up to take my leave, I took from my pocket some chocolate bars and other sweets I had brought along.
"Oh, Monsieur!" cried Jeanne, "there's enough there for the whole boarding house."'
(Anatole France, *Le Crime de Sylvestre Bonnard*, 1881)

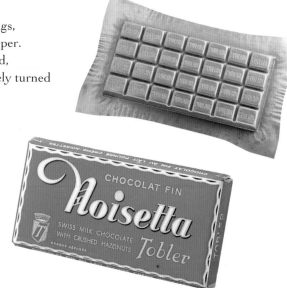

filling is added – a cream, praline or some other filling like those used for individual chocolates. After cooling again, a layer of chocolate is spread over the moulds to form the base of the bar.

**Above:**
After grinding, the bars are cooled in a cooling room.

**Right:**
The modest business set up by Philippe Suchard at Serrières, Switzerland, in 1826 expanded considerably at the end of the 19th century when factories were built at Loerrach in Germany (1880), Bludenz in Austria (1899), Paris (1904), and San Sebastian in Spain (1912). For a long time it was the largest Swiss cocoa maker.

# A memory of chocolate

'Then, as though touching her waist had reminded her of something, she felt in the pocket of her overalls and produced a small slab of chocolate. She broke it in half and gave one of the pieces to Winston. Even before he had taken it he knew by the smell that it was very unusual chocolate. It was dark and shiny, and was wrapped in silver paper. Chocolate normally was dull-brown crumbly stuff that tasted, as nearly as one could describe it, like the smoke of a rubbish fire. But at some time or another he had tasted chocolate like the piece she had given him. The first whiff of its scent had stirred up some memory which he could not pin down, but which was powerful and troubling.
[...] The first fragment of chocolate had melted on Winston's tongue. The taste was delightful. But there was still that memory moving round the edges of his consciousness, something strongly felt but not reducible to a definite shape.'
(George Orwell, *1984*, 1950)

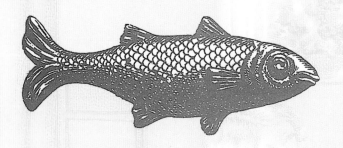

## Moulds of every shape

*B*ecause there are chocolates for every occasion, there is a huge variety of moulds. Coins, letters of the alphabet, historic and legendary figures, flowers, fruits, animals, shells ... Chocolate makers can give free rein to their imagination, and sometimes it is only a short step from a simple mould to a work of art.

### A French pioneer
The tradition of decorative moulds goes back to the 1830s, when makers started to solidify chocolate in particular shapes. Up to then, when chocolate was not supplied in hand-made rolls or tablets, the shapes were hammered out by hand from square cakes made in moulds. The perfection of an efficient grinding process, and of the mass-production iron moulds, paved the way for the development of moulds. In 1832, Jean-Baptiste Létang, a tinsmith from Dinan, started selling chocolate moulds in Paris, in rue Quincampois. He thus launched the profession of tin mould maker and taught it to others.

### Belated recognition
Until around 1855, the mould makers in Paris virtually had a world

monopoly in this kind of object, and French chocolate makers became specialists in 'fantasy' chocolate. Then Germany began to produce moulds, notably the firm of Hermann Walter, founded in Berlin in 1866, and in the second half of the 19th century, mould factories opened in Italy, Switzerland and Belgium, where the firm of Edmé Dunan, founded in Brussels in

1888, acquired a massive reputation. In England, Birmingham was the capital of tin and the Cadbury brothers won fame in the art of moulding: in 1875, they produced their first chocolate Easter eggs, although J S Fry in Bristol had introduced theirs two years earlier. This aspect of chocolate-making was not really taken seriously for several decades. When the First World War was over, automatic moulding machines became widespread.

### Materials for moulding

At first, moulds were made of wood, but its sensitivity to humidity and lack of polish led to a preference for silver and pewter. The latter was heavy and fragile, and in the 18th century, makers turned to copper and especially tin, which did not oxidise like copper. Then came nickel-plated steel, stainless steel and, closer to our own time, plastic, which took over from metal in mould-making. Moulds became more efficient at the expense of the beauty of the material, and since then the old models have become collector's items.

# Tasty chocolates

*T*here are millions of different individual chocolates, made from every kind of chocolate, in every scent and flavour. Making them by industrial means has the advantage of using extremely high-precision machines, and this keeps handling to a strict minimum. On the other hand, confectionery made by craftsmen makes more use of their priceless creativity and skill. However, although the various materials and ingredients used may not culminate in the same finished products, the methods employed are identical.

# Moulded and coated

*Chocolates appeared in Europe a long time after the drink was introduced, and also a long time after sugar confectionery. They were gradually perfected in the 19th century, then in the 20th century basic recipes were established which gave free rein to the makers' imagination.*

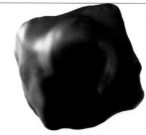

### THE QUALITY OF THE COATING

All chocolates, whether moulded or coated, are made with a covering of chocolate, the composition of which is rigorously controlled by legislation and includes a higher cocoa butter content than ordinary chocolate. This richness in fat content gives them a viscosity which helps to shape them and gives them a sheen that is retained in the finished chocolates. It is worth noting that the cocoa butter content required for a mould (30 to 32%) is different from that for a coating (up to 40%), which produces a difference in consistency; the coating for moulds is less fluid than the other kind. As in the making of tablets or bars, it has to go through a temperature-control stage. The coating is treated in the same way as described earlier, and can then be worked.

### THE TECHNIQUE FOR SOLID CHOCOLATE

Moulds are used a great deal in industrial chocolate-making; large numbers are produced and must conform to the prescribed shape. The manufacturing method is similar to that for filled bars. Enormous production lines carry out the successive operations, guaranteeing

If the departments carrying out the moulding, coating, piping and dragée making are kept at about 20 to 23°C (68 to 73°F), and free of humidity, which is chocolate's worst enemy, the chocolates should then be stored at a temperature of 12 to 15°C (54 to 59°F) until they are packaged.

**Right:**
Pouring a cream filling.

constant patterns and proportions that never deviate. In the hand-made field, moulds are used for chocolates with smooth fillings such as creams, and certain specialities.

### CRAFT SKILLS

The coating process involves making a shape for the filling, for pralines for example, and cutting out the centres in the shape of the chocolates required. Industrial production has stampers to cut out the paste and automatic coaters to cover the insides with liquid chocolate. This is often still done manually for hand-made chocolates, or with coaters which allow the chocolate maker to perform his alchemical magic. Every artist has his secret way of making a fine coating, with a perfect aroma and taste, not too bitter and not too sweet, one that enhances the filling without losing its own identity, and has a lovely velvety colour that just asks to be eaten.

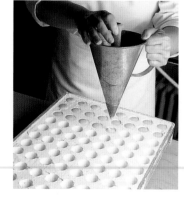

### LIKE IN THE OLD DAYS

Once the filling and coating are right, the two have to be put together, either by applying the coating as before, or by dipping it by hand, which makes for attractive but less uniform products.

This is the oldest method. It is used for difficult fillings such as fruit liqueurs. The filling is immersed in the coating, using a special small fork or a dipping ring, and when it is well coated it is placed on a tray to cool. Once the coating is finished, patterns are inscribed on the chocolates with a fork or a small garnish is added (a nut, almond, coffee bean, etc).

## OTHER PRACTICES

When the chocolate paste is rich enough not to need coating with chocolate, it is decorated with a piping nozzle by putting the paste in a conical cloth holder with a serrated or smooth end, then pressing and turning in order to model the chocolates.

Finally, chocolate makers use turbines to make chocolate dragées with dried fruit (almonds, nuts) or pieces of nougatine.

### Recipe for home-made orange aiguillettes

500 g (20 oz) crystallised orange slices, 100 g (3½ oz) icing sugar, 30 g (1 oz) chopped and grilled almonds, 400 g (14 oz) bitter coating chocolate.

Cut the orange slices lengthways into thin strips. Dip into icing sugar and coat well. Place on a grid and leave to dry for 4 to 5 hours.

Prepare the chocolate coating in a stainless steel pan. Add the almonds. Then, with a fork, dip the orange strips in the mixture. Take care, on removing them, to remove excess chocolate by tapping the back of the fork on the edge of the pan.

Place the coated strips on a sheet of greaseproof paper (or plastic). Leave to cool for a few moments.

(Recipe by Louis Chavanette, Orléans)

# Chocolate fillings

*Fillings are made from a careful selection of almonds, nuts, crystallised fruit, honey, spirits, etc, and then these basic materials are transformed into a filling which has a perfect consistency and unites totally with the chocolate coating. Fillings make the chocolate, and in so doing justify their price. Their nature also determines the way the chocolates are kept.*

**A SURPRISING ALCHEMY**

Fillings made from liqueurs have to be made in a very particular way. This is carried out in special containers. Cavities are hollowed out in a layer of soft starch, and a sweet syrup with alcohol added, or the selected liqueur, is poured into them. On contact with the starch, the sugar crystallises into a fine impermeable 'crust' which adopts the shape of the cavity and, after one or two days, these capsules filled with the liqueur can be removed. The starch is taken off with a brush, and the capsule is covered with a chocolate coating. These chocolates need to be eaten quickly or kept in a dry, airy place.

CHOCOLAT GUERIN-BOUTRON

Noisetier

**FRAGILE CHERRIES IN KIRSCH**

These are also made in a very interesting way. The cherries, preserved in alcohol, are carefully stoned, then dipped, one by one, in a kirsch-flavoured or other fondant, which is kept at the desired fluidity by means of a bain-marie. They are then cooled on a tray; the fondant hardens in about an hour and

a half. Then it is covered with the chocolate coating. The chocolates are then left to rest for two weeks. At the end of this period, the fondant will have completely melted from contact with the alcohol still contained in the cherry, giving way to a fruit surrounded by liquid alcohol. A miraculous transformation!

## Cherries in chocolate

40 cherries in brandy, 250 g (9 oz) fondant, 200 g (7 oz) coating chocolate, 40 pastry cases.

Drain the cherries on a grill for 2 to 3 hours. Place the fondant in a bain-marie and stir with a wooden spatula until it becomes fluid. Dip in the cherries, holding them by the stalk, and place them on a sheet of aluminium foil dusted with icing sugar. Leave to dry for a few hours. Break the chocolate in small pieces and soften it in the bain-marie (without stirring). When it is melted, stir into a smooth paste. Dip the cherries in this paste and place them, as you go, in the cases. Let the cherries rest for 4 or 5 days, when the fondant will have become liquid on contact with the cherries.
(Recipe by Chambeau-Fouquet)

### THE GREAT FILLINGS

*Almond paste.* This is made from boiled sugar and finely ground, blanched white almonds. Its best flavours are coffee, pistachio, orange and some liqueurs. This is a difficult filling to keep as the almond paste soon ferments.

*Caramel.* This is made by cooking a mixture of sugar, glucose, whole milk (or crème fraîche) and a flavouring agent (chocolate, coffee, vanilla, etc). It requires skill, as the filling must be delightfully tender.

*Cream.* A mixture of cream, sugar and glucose is made into a fondant by careful cooking, and a flavour added such as vanilla, coffee, kirsch or some other liqueur. Its texture is soft and not easy to keep.

**Below:**
Adding the warm cream to the chocolate to make ganache.

*Crunchy fillings.* These fillings, very popular with Swiss chocolate makers, are made of melted sugar with ground nuts or almonds added.

*Fondant.* This is a very delicate filling, made from a mixture of sugar and glucose with additional flavourings.

*Ganache.* This requires roughly equal amounts of crème fraîche and chocolate, mixed together and heated, its fluidity varying according to the shape it is given; it is often flavoured with coffee, tea and liqueurs. It is very tricky to keep and never lasts long.

## Cream-filled chocolates

250 g (9 oz) coating chocolate, 50 to 75 g (1¾ to 2½ oz) cocoa butter, 20 g (¾ oz) butter, oil, 10 g (¼ oz) powdered sugar, 1 half pod vanilla. Make a syrup with the sugar, half a glass water and the vanilla. Halfway through the fast boil, add the butter. When the syrup is cooked, pour it on an oiled marble surface and beat until it turns white and thick as a cream. Now divide into small balls the size of a nut, and set aside to air on a plate.

Finely grate the chocolate and melt it in a bain-marie. Slowly add the cocoa butter. The chocolate must be liquid and run freely from the spoon.

Using a pin, dip the cream balls briefly, one by one, in the melted chocolate, then place them as you go on a sheet of paper. Leave to cool.

**Above:** Making almond paste.

**Right:** Making praline.

*Gianduja.* This paste consists of milk chocolate and finely ground hazelnuts in proportions determined by the flavour desired; it is sensitive to heat and difficult to keep. In France, chocolate with hazelnut gianduja is regulated by law. The product obtained from the chocolate must have a minimum content of dry cocoa matter of 32% and that of the dry skimmed cocoa must be 18%, with a cocoa butter content of at least 18%.

*Nougat.* This is made of sugar and honey, lightened with egg white and garnished with dried fruits (sweet almonds, nuts or pistachios). Nougat used as a chocolate filling must be smoother than nougat eaten as a delicacy by itself. In Germany, the term *nougat* means praline.

*Nougatine.* This mixture of caramelised sugar and split almonds, sometimes flavoured with vanilla, can be used alone or mixed with praline. Its enemy is humidity, which destroys its friability and makes it soft and tasteless.

*Praline.* This is considered to be one of the finest fillings;

The praline is poured into
a dish and then smoothed.

it owes its fine taste to the quality of the dried
fruits used and its smoothness after gentle cooking.

It is made from equal
amounts of sugar and
dried fruits. The dried
fruits can be almonds
or nuts by themselves
or mixed together.
The sugar and dried
fruit mixture is cooked
on a low heat, then
ground fairly finely
depending on the
consistency desired.
The addition of
coating chocolate
then gives it a finer
texture which can
be worked.

# A thousand and one chocolates

*Chocolate makers are always trying to create new shapes and flavours. Their efforts are guided both by changing tastes and by local traditions.*

## NATIONAL AND REGIONAL INFLUENCES

Manufacturers are often inspired by the products of their countries and add them to their repertoire. At other times, a historic or remarkable event may trigger a new chocolate, or perhaps the memory of a place, a building or a celebrity. There are so many sources of inspiration for inventive chocolate makers, all of whom have their own range of specialities.

**Above:**
In Angers, the Carreau des Rairies is shaped like the terracotta tiles found in the region. It is a balanced mixture of orange-flavoured almond paste and praline with Cointreau, coated in chocolate the colour of baked clay.

## MUSE NUMBER ONE: NATURE

In France, the name and the shape often go together. *Chardons* (thistles), made of white chocolate in different colour combinations, belong really to the Alps, but also to other non-mountainous regions, which flavour them with their local spirit. *Glaçons* (ice cubes) are associated with the mountains and often consist of nut pralines with crushed nougatine under a coating of ivory chocolate, while *Snowballs* contain almond praline and nuts under an ivory chocolate coating dusted with sugar. Names like

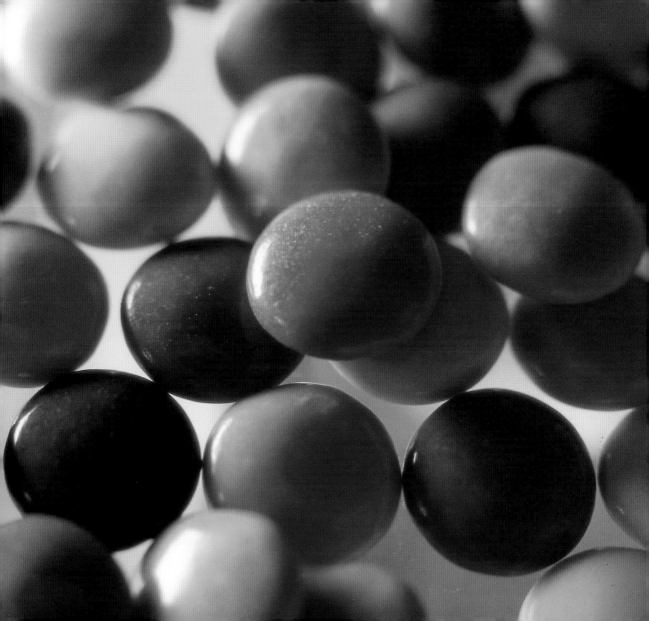

## Spider illusion

*Roc* and *Rocaille* evoke rocky landscapes. *Roseaux* (reeds) are little sticks of nougatine coated in chocolate or small chocolate batons filled with alcohol and represent landscapes with rivers. *Branches* and *Bûches* (logs), filled with flaky layers and nougatine, are made in woodland areas.

### PRODUCTS OF THE LAND

*Sarments* (vine shoots), elongated chocolates often filled with an old local spirit, are a delicacy in wine-producing regions. These regions also produce *Bouchons* (corks), which have a praline filling; in Champagne and Bordeaux they are a speciality. Local products of both land and sea are often commemorated in a special chocolate. *Oysters* are from the seaside, like various other kinds of shell-shaped chocolates. You can always find *Escargots* (snails) in Burgundy – they are a great speciality in Dijon – and also in Poitou. We could mention many

**Right:**
Cutting up the soft chocolate caramel to make fillings.

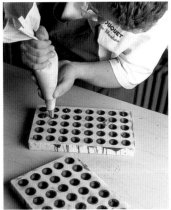

other well-known foods whose shapes have inspired
chocolate makers.

### CLASSIC CHOCOLATES: AN A TO Z

The name describes the shape, the filling and the flavour.

*Bar.* The popular long bar, with a variety of fillings and
flavours (coconut, nougat, caramel, wafer, biscuit,
cereal, etc).

*Baton.* Unlike chocolate bars, these have fillings like those
of individual chocolates.

*Chocolates.* The generic name for chocolate confectionery.
Individual chocolates usually weigh between 9 and 12 g
(¼ and ½ oz). If they are coated or moulded,
the weight of the covering varies, but an ideal
proportion is 30% of the chocolate's total weight.

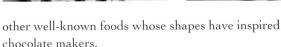

*Bouchée.* Literally a 'mouthful', these are designed
to be eaten whole. The fillings are the same as for
chocolates. Note: in Switzerland, a *bouchée de
chocolat* is the term for an ordinary chocolate.

## Recipes for truffles

**125 g (4 oz) block of dark chocolate, 125 g (4 oz) split grilled almonds, 125 g (4 oz) powdered sugar, crystallised sugar, 1 pinch powdered vanilla. Grate the chocolate. Put the chocolate, almonds, sugar and vanilla in a salad bowl. Add 2 soup spoons cold water. Mix well, stirring with a wooden spatula for about 10 minutes. Shape the mixture into small balls, then roll in crystallised sugar. Leave to dry for half an hour. Keep in an air-tight tin.**

Classic chocolates such as pralines and truffles can be found in all regions; they may be dark, white or coloured, and often flavoured with a liqueur from the local vintage.

*Candy.* Generic term used in the USA to describe sweets and chocolates.

A *candy bar* usually has a filling.

*Cigarettes.* Used for decorating cakes and ice creams. Cocoa butter is added to coating chocolate and rolled into 'cigarettes'.

*Cream.* General word for chocolates filled with a flavoured cream or fondant.

*Croquette.* A small chocolate disc.

*Croissant.* Crystallised orange peel dipped in an orange fondant and coated with chocolate.

*Crunch.* A nut, often a hazelnut, dipped in praline and covered with coating chocolate.

*Dragée.* A small flat disc of chocolate, often used for decorating cakes.

*Griotte.* Word also used to describe Cherries in Chocolate (see recipe, page 88).

*Hundreds and thousands.* Chocolate granules used to decorate desserts and ice creams.

*Latte.* Borrowed from the fashionable coffee drink to describe a coffee-flavoured ganache coated with milk chocolate.

*Orangette.* Crystallised orange peel coated in chocolate.

*Palet d'or.* These 'golden discs' are specialities with a ganache filling, often flavoured with fine champagne or coffee and much enjoyed by chocolate lovers.

*Pastille.* This is also a disc-shaped chocolate, but has no filling. It is named after its inventor, the Florentine confectioner Giovanni Pastilla, who was in Maria de' Medici's entourage when she went to the French court to marry King Henri IV.

*Truffle.* This chocolate has a ganache filling coated with unsweetened cocoa powder.

*Whirl.* Term used in industrial chocolate-making to describe a top-shaped chocolate with spiralling grooves around the sides; a speciality of British and US manufacturers.

'Rivers of milk, chocolate rocks and other such things. The idea is this: you live without working, and nature supplies everything. Often we seek far and wide for what is right before us; the land of milk and honey is right before us; it's the life of a child.'
**(Alain, *Les Dieux*, II)**

**Above left:**
In the 1950s, the industrial world produced these little buttons which delighted children and adults everywhere.

**Right:**
Angers has pretty slate-roofed houses and covers its chocolates in the same colour. The *Quernons d'Ardoise* blend the slight bitterness of the chocolate with the sweet flavour of nougatine.

# How to keep chocolate

### RULES FOR GOOD HOUSEKEEPING

In the 18th century, it became the custom to wrap chocolate in grey paper, then place it in a box within a box. In the following century, they put it in tinfoil. Today, chocolate is packaged at a temperature between 15 and 20°C (59 and 68°F), the ideal being 18°C (64°F). Large variations in temperature must be strictly avoided, otherwise a whitish frost appears on the surface; the attack is only on the outside, however, and does not affect the quality. This greyish look also appears when chocolates are kept in the refrigerator, which is clearly not recommended. It is just as important that chocolate should be protected from smells, dust, smoke, etc. It should not be exposed to light, or the sugar crystallises on the surface and the chocolate acquires a stale taste. Similarly, it should kept free of humidity; the ideal hygrometric level is around 55%. The keeping time varies between six to eight months for milk chocolate and specialities with fillings, and a year and a half for dark chocolate. If you eat it within two months, it will still be at its best.

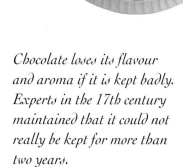

*Chocolate loses its flavour and aroma if it is kept badly. Experts in the 17th century maintained that it could not really be kept for more than two years.*

Bear in mind that some fillings keep better than others. Praline keeps well, but liqueur fillings are more tricky.

## GOOD QUALITY PAYS

The lower the quality of the chocolate, the more difficult it is to keep. A good chocolate has a smooth surface with a silky sheen and is free of stains. When it is broken, the noise should be dry and the breakage clean, with no rough edges. All chocolate that crumbles, or looks sandy in section, is too old or does not contain enough cocoa buter. It is also too old if it bends instead of breaking. Similarly, a milk chocolate that can be stretched is deficient in cocoa butter. Quality can best be judged by the aroma, which should be delicate and sustained. Finally, chocolate should melt on the tongue. Smoothness and a subtle taste are the mark of a balanced product.

## A kind of masterpiece

They turn out Easter eggs, Father Christmases, St Nicholases, all sorts of animals – from rabbits to fish – or simply chocolate bars with bas-relief motifs on various subjects. However, far from being content with these traditional mouldings that they are obliged to produce for special occasions and various other celebrations, some chocolate makers try to express their professional skill by making works of art in chocolate, just as the Compagnons du Tour de France have to design a 'masterpiece'. Their creative talents inspire them to work in chocolate with the same inventive power as someone

# Artists in chocolate

*C*hocolate is like sugar. It can be modelled, and chocolate makers can be artists.

would apply to one of the materials used to make sculptures.

## Real architects

They build cathedrals and castles, faithful reconstructions or pure products of the imagination. From the Palace of Versailles to a new office building like the Gherkin in London, no architecture

LE CHATEAU DE CHOCOLAT

CONTE DE YETTE LAFORAT
IMAGES DE VATIN

'Following their guides, they arrived at a large château, made entirely of chocolate ... Little creatures came to welcome them, including the goblin of chocolate. 'The château belongs to me,' he told them. 'You are my prisoners. You will stay here! You will be condemned to eat cakes and chocolates for ever! For ever!'
(Tale by Yette Laforat)

can resist the fluidity of chocolate, which can be used with great precision. People and animals come to life. Everyday or fantasy objects can be modelled. And now that there are different coloured chocolates, the palette of possibilities is endless. This marginal activity, which unfortunately figures too often in competitions for prizes organised all over the place, has produced the most sophisticated structures as well as the most extravagant works. But whether the results are highly realistic or rather more outrageous, there is always something ephemeral about these sculptures, however artistic they may be. They should be praised for that, too, for it is rare to find artists who accept that there is no eternity.

# The uses of chocolate

There are chocophiles, chocomaniacs, wholehearted munchers, inveterate consumers, and so on. Chocolate has its admirers, its fans and its clubs. In the kingdom of delicacies, it reigns as the undisputed master. But gradually it has made itself felt in the world of desserts and pastries, to a point where it has become indispensable. Even the sectarian world of savouries has found a place for it.

# Drinking chocolate

'It was smooth and silky, and just from seeing it being poured from the chocolate pot, you could guess it would caress its way onto the tongue and palate.'
(James de Coquet, Propos de Table, 1964)

**Below:**
Engraving from *New and Curious Essays on Coffee, Tea and Chocolate*, by Philippe Sylvestre Dufour (1685).

## CHOCOLATE AS IT USED TO BE

Thanks to texts dating from the 17th century, we know the recipes the Amerindians used to make chocolate before the Spanish Conquest. The main ingredients were: beans from the coconut tree or Indian palm, grilled with cocoa beans; nuts, also grilled; a generous portion of *atolli*, a maize gruel; orejevala flowers, dried and pulverised, and finally *achiolt* or *rocou*, a sap from a fruit tree, which gave the mixture a red colour. It was all dissolved in hot water to produce a drink with a lot of froth. The addition of powdered and sieved sugar, mentioned in texts of the time, did not happen until the Spanish arrived in America. Rich men and dignitaries consumed this drink, without *atolli*, 'seasoned with vanilla-flavoured honey, or mixed with green maize, *octli* (fermented agave juice) or peppers' (Jacques Soustelle).

## IMPROVED CHOCOLATE

The Spanish could not adapt to the taste, so they quickly changed the way it was made. They added sugar to the cocoa, to reduce its bitterness, vanilla to improve the taste, and a little Indian pepper, which the Spanish called

Chocolat Express
Grondard Paris
PAS MÊME DEUX MINUTES!!!

## Chinese chocolate

'Take some well roasted and winnowed cocoa and grind it carefully, mix in 120 g (4 oz) cocoa kernels, 30 g (1 oz) vanilla, 30 g (1 oz) fine cinnamon, a small amount of ambergris and 30 g (1 oz) powdered sugar. Make this into a paste put it in a tin box; if you want to give your chocolate a pleasant flavour, add in ten to twelve grains of this mixture, which is excellent and good for restoring strength after exhaustion. The Chinese make much use of this paste and are very happy with it.' This recipe, provided by Alexandre Dumas in his *Grand Dictionnaire de Cuisine*, is probably one of the most invigorating. It is more doubtful that the Chinese often used it, as chocolate is fairly rare in Asia.

MELROSE Régénérateur favori des CHEVEUX.

*chilé* and which gave the chocolate an acrid and spicy taste. Later the inhabitants of New Spain added cinnamon and cloves. This was the recipe that became most widely taken up in France in the 17th century: cocoa, sugar, vanilla, cinnamon, cloves, ambergris and musk; the French did not like the taste of the pepper and left it out. Some even added cardamom and ginger in tiny doses, others a little orange flower water.

### Hot chocolate

Thus the Europeans increased the number of ingredients. This can be explained by the fact that, until they started to extract the fatty matter, the drink was heavy and fatty, and aromas and perfumes had to be added to it to make it drinkable.

Again, although some Indians drank it cold, the Europeans adopted the habit of drinking hot chocolate. Only the Italians liked it in 'iced' form. Nicolas de Blégny was against this, wanting chocolate to be 'as hot as possible' so that it would not be noxious to the stomach. According to Thomas Gage, the most common way of preparing it was 'to heat the water well, then fill half the drinking cup and dissolve one or, at the most, two tablets in it until the water was sufficiently thick, then stir it well with a spoon, and when it was well beaten and turned to foam, to fill the cup with hot water and drink it, after adding sugar as needed, and eat a little jam or marzipan dipped in the chocolate'.

### CHOCOLATE WITH MILK

Although custom required the chocolate to be mixed with water, in the 18th century some people began to prefer milk. This change is attributed to Sir Hans Sloane, President of the Royal Society, who had discovered the nutritional properties of chocolate on a voyage to Jamaica; this contributed to the rise of chocolate-drinking in England. In the Age of Enlightenment, chocolate was made in different ways in different countries. In Mexico, the Spanish continued the old tradition with a composition made of cocoa, sugar, pepper, *achiolt* and vanilla, some people adding cinnamon, cloves or

'Chocolate hangs in the air, a silver sun plays in my cup.' (Colette, *La Retraite Sentimentale*.)

**Above:**
For a long time, advertisements for Cacao Van Houten stressed the lower cost of cocoa compared with chocolate, and how easy it was to make.

aniseed, even ambergris and musk. In the French West Indies, they reduced the skimmed cocoa cakes to a fine powder, added sugar to it then mixed this with a fresh egg and poured hot water or milk on it. The height of refinement was in Martinique, where the English soaked the egg first in Madeira wine. In Spain, the recipe was like the one used by the Spanish in Mexico. Finally, in France, chocolate was prepared without embellishments, much as we drink it today. Only cinnamon and vanilla were at all favoured by the discerning French.

## PERFECTING RECIPES

From the 19th century, recipes gradually became more refined. Cocoa, sugar and cinnamon were the most popular combination. When people started to prefer cream to milk, chocolate was made with cream: first it was melted in hot cream on a low heat, with constant stirring. A simpler solution was to add a spoonful of fresh cream to each cup. Almond-flavoured chocolate was chocolate with cream, with a little almond

syrup added on serving.
Chocolate with eggs
consisted of chocolate
à la crème with an egg yolk
beaten with sugar.

### RECIPES TODAY

Methods for making real
chocolate have not changed,
either with milk
or water, with
cocoa powder
or tablets of
dark chocolate.
For Vienna-
style chocolate,
you add half
an egg yolk
per cup,
letting it thicken on a low heat and putting
a spoonful of whipped cream on top of each cup. Javan
chocolate combines equal parts of coffee and bitter chocolate,
with sugar added according to taste. For Brazilian-style
coffee, made with sweetened milk, add half a cup of very
strong coffee per litre of chocolate. Cinnamon and cloves
add their own aromas too, and rum or cherry brandy
may also be used to enhance the flavour. There are
aromas for all tastes. It is just a pity that people no
longer use chocolate pots.

'No chocolate is better prepared, or
made with such pure ingredients, or
sold more cheaply than Chocolat des
Gourmets.' Typical advertising copy
from the Belle Époque.

## According to
## Brillat-Savarin ...

'To make chocolate, that is, to
make it for immediate consumption, take about an ounce and a
half per cup and dissolve gently
in water as it is heating, stirring
with a wooden spatula; boil it
for a quarter of an hour so
that it gains consistency, and
serve hot.
Madame d'Arestel was Mother
Superior at the Convent of the
Visitation in Belley. Monsieur,
she said to me more than fifty
years ago, if you want to have
good chocolate, make it the
previous evening in an earthen-
ware cafetière and leave it.
Resting overnight concentrates it
and gives it a smoothness which
makes it much better. The Good
Lord cannot be offended by this
little refinement, for it is such an
excellent thing.'
(*Physiology of Taste*, 1825)

# Elegant containers

*There could not have been real chocolate without chocolate pots, which came into existence at the same time as the drink they were destined to contain.*

### Pre-Columbian origins

The word 'chocolate' is said to come from the old Mexican *chocoatl* or *chocollatl* (sources vary on this), which in turn came from *choco*, 'sound', and *atl* or *latté*, 'water'. This recalled the sound caused by the stirrer used by the pre-Columbians to whip up the drink before it was served.

The Conquest and the adoption of chocolate by the Spanish altered nothing in the way it was prepared. 'A stick in the shape of the spindle with which they twist yarn in Spain,' was how in 1618 Barthelemy Marradon described the stirrer used by Indian women together with the apastlet, 'a vessel like a terrine', to prepare chocolate in the market-places of New Spain.

**Left:**
A chocolate pot from the beginning of the 20th century.

**IMPLEMENTS FOR CHOCOLATE DRINKING**

These utensils were introduced to Europe along with chocolate, and were adapted to suit the aesthetics of our civilisation. In 1687, Nicolas de Blégny was already describing the container familiar to us today: 'To prepare this drink, they generally use containers like cafetières, the one difference being that those

Chocolat Poulain
Goutez et comparez! Qualité sans Rivale

used for chocolate, and known as chocolate pots, have a hole in the middle of the lid for the handle of the stirrer, [...] which is fairly useless as it is neither necessary not convenient to keep the chocolate covered while using the stirrer.' The lid was not entirely superfluous, however, as it helped to keep the drink hot while it was being whipped. In the second half of the 17th century, when chocolate was much in vogue, it was unthinkable to make it any way other than in a chocolate pot.

# The old way

'You put in enough water for the portions you want to make and, having placed it on the heat, you add an ounce of grated chocolate for each portion as soon as it begins to boil. If there is not enough sugar in the chocolate, you can add a nut's worth to each cup, let it boil up three times, then move it off the heat a little and let it simmer for a quarter of an hour. When you are ready to pour it into the cups, you stir it with the stirrer, which is a little mace of boxwood, the head of which is carved and indented, and a handle long enough to whip up the liquor to a good froth [...] You carry on doing this after removing the chocolate pot from the heat, until it is good and frothy; you pour this froth into the cup or goblet, and top it up with the rest of the mixture. You keep on stirring to make more froth, and then you fill the other cups until the chocolate pot is empty.'
(Massialot, 1732)

## Chocolate time

'The Creole woman always had a basket full of delicacies for her nephew, who ruined his teeth sucking sweets and eating over-sugary pastries. Every day, when she only had Johnny with her, she brought out a kind of travelling kitchen. It was a little trunk in fine leather, lined with silvered metal; it contained a portable stove, a silver teapot, a chocolate pot, silver cups and saucers, spoons, porcelain bowls for the sandwiches and the butter, tins for the sugar, choco-late, tea, embroidered napkins, and a large straight bottle for the milk. There were so many things, it was like a conjuror's box. [...]
'What have you got for us?' asked Fermina in her firm, nonchalant manner.
Pilar mimed rolling a spatula between her hands in a chocolate pot.'
(Valery Larbaud, *Fermina Marquez*, 1926)

### A REFINED OBJECT

The chocolate pot developed along the same lines as chocolate, starting as a luxury object and becoming accessible to more people. At first it was made of precious metal or fine porcelain and, together with the cafetière and the teapot, joined the other accoutrements of society at court and among the nobility. This happened regardless of country. Thus we find, among the gifts brought by Siamese ambassadors to the French court in 1686, 'two silver chocolate pots with gold flowers' intended for the Dauphin and Dauphine. It was evidently the done thing to honour eating and drinking.

### THE TABLES OF FASHIONABLE SOCIETY

In the following century, the fashion

for chocolate pots was even greater. It acquired its final silhouette, a slender and elegant shape. Goldsmiths and porcelain manufacturers vied with each other and made their mark. The Marquise de Pompadour is said to have been the first to order a chocolate service from the Sèvres factory. Meissen, in eastern Germany, brought out some of the finest pieces known to us. Silver pots were the province of, notably, the French masters Jean-Baptiste François Chéret, Guillaume Pigeron and Martin-Guillaume Biennais, who made some remarkable versions.

### GRANDEUR AND DECADENCE

As chocolate reached an ever-wider public, chocolate pots kept their original shape but were more simply made. In the 18th century, copper chocolate pots appeared, intended for middle-class or more modest households. This did not last long, as copperware was killed off by kitchen utensils made of hammered iron and tin. However, whether it was made of metal or porcelain, the tradition of serving foaming chocolate in special pots survived until the Belle Époque. Then, like many other utensils linked to a way of life that faded away, it gradually disappeared. Today it is rare to find people using a chocolate pot unless their interest is as much that of a collector as of a chocolate-drinker.

**Left:**
Engraving from Nicolas de Blégny's work *The Good Use of Tea, Coffee and Chocolate for Keeping It and Curing Illnesses* (Paris, 1687), with stirrers in various shapes for whipping chocolate. As the author wrote, the stirrer was 'a kind of little mace of boxwood, the head of which is chiselled in various ways, and the handle or stick fairly long compared to the size of the head, which needs almost to fill the opening in the chocolate pot.'

# Chocolate in gastronomy

*'Chocolate used in the culinary arts is the kind that would win the most support and unanimous praise from gastronomes who gain great enjoyment from liqueurs, ices, creams and other seasonings which go so well with chocolate.'*
*(E Delcher, 1857)*

## FAMILIAR PREPARATIONS

Chocolate, used as an icing or decorative element, has become one of the favourite ingredients of sweet dishes. There are many recipes for the famous chocolate mousse. Chocolate sauce accompanies many desserts. Pear Belle-Hélène is topped with warm chocolate. *Nègre en chemise* is a chocolate dish topped with Chantilly cream. Éclairs are made with chocolate confectioner's custard and coated with chocolate, like iced cream puffs. Profiteroles offer the contrast of something cold, with the ice cream inside the pastry, and the warm bitter chocolate poured over them. Charlottes and bavarois can be made with chocolate. Black Forest gâteau, probably originating from east of the Rhine, is rich in chocolate, garnished with whipped cream and crystallised cherries. Ice creams include chocolate ices (with eggs and butter), ices made from unsweetened cocoa powder and parfaits. The fashion for fondues also now includes the chocolate fondue, served with chopped fresh fruit. Not to mention pancakes, waffles, meringues, chocolate soufflés, etc.

## Cocoa cream

Cocoa beans are used as a flavouring in the apéritif Cap Corse. Advocaat, an egg liqueur from Holland, is sometimes flavoured with chocolate. But mainly cocoa is used to make a syrupy liqueur. The beans are roasted and crushed, and infused with a neutral spirit. Alcohol derived from another distilled spirit is then added. Vanilla is often used as a flavouring. Makers of cocoa cream generally call it *chouao* or *chouva*, from the estate in the West Indies which used to supply the beans.

Crême de CACAO

**DESSERTS OF EVERY KIND** Following France's lead, every country now includes chocolate among its specialities. There is no point in listing them here, because the list of cakes and biscuits using this ingredient is endless. We will limit ourselves to a brief survey of these sweets, noting meanwhile that Africa and Asia have not embraced chocolate in their diet, whereas in Europe it is found everywhere. In England, chocolate puddings are topped with chocolate sauce. In Italy, zabaglione can be made with chocolate. Their *torta al cioccolate* (chocolate tart) is very popular. Some ice creams (*gelati*), based on milk, are flavoured with chocolate. In the Ancona region, they make ravioli stuffed with chocolate. Around Ferrara, they make a *pan pepato di cioccolato*, a sort of chocolate brioche with spices and almonds, topped with chocolate and decorated with little chocolates, which they eat on New Year's Eve. In Sweden, the *hovdessert* is a meringue with chocolate cream and fresh cream. In Denmark, the *chocoladefromage* is a chocolate dessert. In Germany, they like their chocolate cakes. In Austria, as well as *Indianerkrapfen*, made of pastry garnished with chocolate-flavoured

The famous Austrian *Sacher Torte*.

whipped cream, the most famous pastry is the *Sacher Torte*. The Poles coat their babas with chocolate, and love making chocolate tarts, while the Romanians make a very thick sort of jam based on chocolate.

## ACROSS THE ATLANTIC

In Mexico they keep up their chocolate tradition with, among others, a chocolate pie. In the West Indies, they make a marvellous blend of chocolate and pineapple. Until the 19th century, it seems, crystallised cocoa was very popular: the beans were picked before they were ripe and crystallised in variously flavoured syrups (lemon, cinnamon, musk, ambergris, etc). In the United States, they have chocolate cookies, and devil's food cake is a very popular chocolate cake. In his book *The Chocolate Cookbook* (1967), William I Kaufman mentions an old traditional recipe for a pancake in butter, which is very popular in New England and now includes little pieces of chocolate.

Fameuse, cette crème au chocolat!

CRÈME AU CHOCOLAT préparée par le LAIT MONT BLANC *toujours prête toujours parfaite*

**Above:**
One of the treats of the 1950s: advertisement on a place mat. Sweet gâteaux and those with 'creams perfumed with ambergris', for which Des Esseintes, the hero of Huysmans' novel *Against Nature*, had a weakness ... In the 19th century, chocolate was included in the makeup of many desserts.

# Unusual blends

*We have to go to Mexico, where it first came from, and then, obviously enough, Spain to find the first unlikely combinations of sweet and savoury that involved the use of chocolate.*

## TRADITIONAL RECIPES

The best-known preparation is the *mole* or turkey in chocolate. The sauce is made from several spices, chocolate, almonds and banana. This Mexican speciality came from the state of Puebla, and is eaten at festivals. A legend has it that the recipe for it was created, at the time of the Spanish occupation, by nuns from the Convent of Santa Rosa in Puebla, on the occasion of a visit by their archbishop. In fact, though, this dish was already known at the court of the Aztec emperor, and Hernán Cortés was invited there to try it. However that may be, thanks to the nuns of Puebla, the recipe has been handed down, the only change being to replace the exotic condiments with more everyday spices. Other meats linked with chocolate are chicken and pork. The sauce is made in the same way as for the turkey. In Spain we also find braised rabbit in chocolate; this is simmered in full-bodied red wine, with added herbs; chocolate and almonds enhance the flavour.

## A CHEF'S RECIPE

This kind of recipe first appeared in France in the 17th century, but is no longer used. An example is the recipe supplied by Massialot in *Le Cuisinier Roïal et Bourgeois* (1691): 'Duck in chocolate. After plucking and cleaning your duck, wash it and blanch it on the

stove, then put it in a pot, season it with
salt, pepper, bay and a bouquet garni: make some chocolate
and pour it in. At the same time, prepare a ragout with the
liver, mushrooms, morels, meadow mushrooms, truffles
and a handful of chestnuts. When
your duck is cooked and put out
on a dish, pour your ragout over it,
and serve it with whatever garnish
you wish.'
This was the only Aztec recipe
published in France at that time.
The chocolate was used as a
thickening agent.

### USED AS AN ACCOMPANIMENT

As a delicacy, chocolate is sufficient
by itself, whether dark or milk,
filled or not. It loses its flavour if
it is consumed at the same time as
a drink. However, you can put a
liqueur inside a shell of chocolate,
or coat an orange- or mint-flavoured
filling. The spirit then bonds with
the chocolate, and the flavour is
assimilated into the overall taste
of the chocolate. Keeping two
tastes separate reduces their value.
The only drinks which can tolerate
this kind of combination are
fortified wines, particularly port,
also champagne and, possibly, sweet
wines and liqueurs.

Coffee goes very well with chocolate
and is even improved by it. There is
nothing better than truffles eaten with
a cup of hot coffee.

# Chocolate drinks of yesterday and today

*N̄escao, the 'breakfast for children and parents', Phoscao for 'an exquisite breakfast – it builds up your strength', Ovaltine, 'the modern fortifying food', Banania, 'the best of all starts to the morning'.*

### Nutritious sources of energy

Chocolate drinks recall childhood and breakfasts accompanied by a delicious aroma of cocoa. A fragrance from the past in a series of Proustian remembrances! In the last few decades, these instant powders which combine cocoa (20% on average) with various additives such as banana powder and malt extract now have to compete with cereals, drinking yoghurts and flavoured milks. They have lost some of their popularity, but they still go on today, using the same basic recipe adapted slightly to suit fashionable tastes and flavours such as coconut. Now there's something for gourmands!

**Right:**
Advertising plaque designed by Thebault in 1940 for Nescao, a breakfast drink made by Nestlé containing cocoa, milk, sugar and malted wheat biscuit.

### In France: Banania

One of the most famous of the chocolate-flavoured powders, Banania, was created in 1912 when a pharmacist from Courbevoie had the idea of combining banana powder with a mixture of cocoa, sugar and barley sugar. The first advertisement for the product (1914) showed a West Indian woman surrounded by bananas and bringing 'vigour, energy,

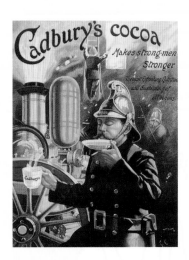

### In England: Cadbury's cocoa and drinking chocolate

Cocoa and drinking chocolate had been introduced into England in the 1650s. At first they were luxury items, enjoyed by the elite of society, who were the only people to be able to afford to buy them, but over the centuries they became more accessible to everyone.

On 1st March 1824 the following advertisement appeared in the Birmingham Gazette:

'John Cadbury is desirous of introducing to particular notice "Cocoa Nibs", prepared by himself, an article affording a most nutritious beverage for breakfast'.

Today Cadbury's drinking chocolate is one of the most popular and readily available beverages in Great Britain.

health and power' to a threatened France. But later a legend grew up around the famous slogan 'Y'a bon' (It's good), linked to the brand image of the Senegalese infantryman, created by Severo Pozzati, known as 'Sepo'. Towards the end of the Great War, a wounded soldier was apparently sent to convalesce at the home of the pharmacist who created the product, and, having tasted the new drink, showed his enthusiasm with a 'Y'a bon' which became famous.

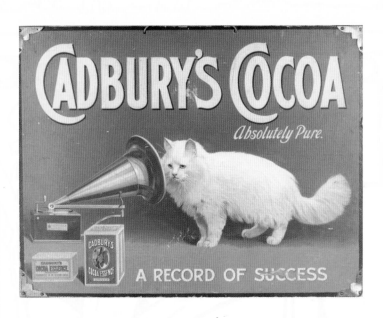

# Some recipes

### Chocolate charlotte

150 g (6 oz) sponge fingers
100 g (4 oz) bitter chocolate
125 g (5 oz) cherry jam
10 g (¼ oz) butter, 3 eggs
100 ml (3½ fl oz) cherry brandy
½ tablespoon milk
75 g (3 oz) caster sugar

Moisten the biscuits in cherry brandy (without soaking them). Spread jam on the insides. Line a buttered charlotte mould with them. In the bain-marie, melt the chocolate in the milk. Add the sugar and

egg yolks. Beat the egg whites until stiff, then add them, away from the heat, to the chocolate mixture. Pour this into the mould. Cover with biscuits, also moistened and covered with jam. Place in the fridge for 12 hours.

### Caramels

80 g (3 oz) coating chocolate
50 g (2 oz) butter
100 ml (3½ fl oz) milk
250 g (9 oz) caster sugar
1 pinch vanilla powder

Dissolve the sugar in half a glass water. In the bain-marie, melt the chocolate in the milk, flavoured earlier with vanilla. Add the butter and bring to the boil. Pour over the sugar.
Place the mixture on a low heat. Stop cooking when a drop of the mixture solidifies on contact with cold water. Pour onto an oiled marble surface and cut immediately into squares.

### Sachertorte

For the tart:
150 g (6 oz) dark chocolate
150 g (6 oz) butter
150 g (6 oz) caster sugar
150 g (6 oz) flour
8 eggs
For the icing:
120 g (4 oz) coating chocolate
150 g (6 oz) apricot jam
250 g (9 oz) icing sugar

Mix the butter (softened) with the chocolate (melted and warm), the egg yolks and 100 g (4 oz) sugar. Beat the egg whites until they are stiff and add the rest of the sugar to them. Add the whites to the chocolate mixture. Add the flour, stirring gently. Pour into a buttered sandwich tin. Cook in the oven (180°C/350°F) for about 50 minutes. Leave to cool and rest for 12 hours. Remove the gâteau and cover with jam. Melt the chocolate and the sugar in 125 ml (4 fl oz) water on a low heat, stirring as you go. Top the gâteau with the icing. Leave to dry.

## Chocolate truffles

85 g (3 oz) coating chocolate
50 g (2 oz) butter
65 g (2½ oz) icing sugar
1 tablespoon milk
granules of drinking chocolate

In the bain-marie, melt the butter and the chocolate (grated beforehand). Then, away from the heat, add the finely sieved icing sugar and the cream of milk. Leave to rest in a cool place for 12 hours.
Roll the paste into small balls. Roll these in the chocolate granules until coated.

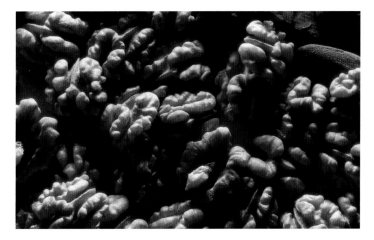

## Ardèche gâteau

500 g (18 oz) chestnuts
100 g (4 oz) drinking chocolate
(or grated chocolate)
100 g (4 oz) butter
500 ml (18 fl oz) milk
100 g (4 oz) caster sugar

Peel the chestnuts and cook them in the milk. Drain and purée. Add the butter, then the sugar and the chocolate. Mix well. Pour the mixture in a buttered cake tin and leave to set in the fridge for 12 hours. Remove from the tin and serve.

## Chocolates with dried fruits

200 g (8 oz) coating chocolate
100 g (4 oz) green walnuts
100 g (4 oz) stoned dates
50 g (2 oz) almonds
50 g (2 oz) butter
½ tablespoon kirsch

Chop the dates. Crush the nuts very finely. Chop the almonds. In the bain-marie, melt the chocolate with a spoonful water. Add the butter, then, away from the heat, the dates, nuts and kirsch. Mix well. Roll the paste into small balls, and roll them in the almonds.

# Further reading

BRODY (Lora): *Chocolate American Style*, Clarkson N Potter Publishers, 2004.

CLARENCE-SMITH (William Gervase): *Cocoa and Chocolate, 1765–1914*, Routledge, 2000.

COADY (Chantal) and Foster (Richard): *Real Chocolate*, Quadrille Publishing, 2004.

COADY (Chantal): *The Chocolate Companion: A Connoiseur's Guide to the World's Finest Chocolates*, Simon & Schuster, 1995.

COE (Sophie D): *The True History of Chocolate*, Thames and Hudson, 2003.

DIVONE (Judene): *Chocolate Moulds: A history & Encyclopedia*, Oakton Hills, 1987.

DUNBAR (Patricia): *Cadbury's Chocolate Cookbook*, Bounty Books, 1993.

GONZALEZ (Elaine) and FRANKENY (Frankie): *The Art of Chocolate: Techniques and Recipes for Simply Spectacular Desserts and Confections*, Chronicle Books, 1998.

LINXE (Robert) and CARLES (Michael): *La Maison du Chocolat*, Rizzoli International Publications, 2000.

PRESILLA (Maricel E): *The New Taste of Chocolate: A Guide to Fine Chocolate with Recipes*, Ten Speed Press, 2001.

RUBINSTEIN (Helge): *The Chocolate Book*, Penguin Books, 1982.

RUNCIE (James): *The Discovery of Chocolate*, HarperCollins, 2001.

SMITH (Delia): *The Delia Collection: Chocolate*, BBC Consumer Publishing, 2003.

TEUBNER (Christian), ed: *The Chocolate Bible*, Book Sales, 2004.

TERRIO (Susan J): *Crafting the Culture and History of French Chocolate*, University of California Press, 2000.

YOUNG (Allen M): *The Chocolate Tree: A Natural History of Cacao*, Smithsonian Books, 1994.

# Specialist shops

There are specialist shops throughout the world selling chocolate. Here is just a small selection.

AUSTRALIA
*Belle Fleur Fine Chocolates*
658 Darling Street, Rozelle,
Sydney, NSW 2039

AUSTRIA
*Heindl Schokowelt*
Willendorfergasse 2–8, 1230 Vienna

BELGIUM
*Burie Chocolatier*
Korte Gasthuisstraat 3, Antwerp
*Chocolaterie Hans De Groote*
Market Square 7, 8900 Ypres
*Mary Chocolatier*
73 Rue Royale, 1000 Brussels

CANADA
*Appleton Chocolates Company*
567 Lake Road, Wentworth,
Nova Scotia B0M 1Z0
*Érico Fine Chocolates*
634 Rue Saint-Jean, Faubourg
Saint-Jean Baptiste, Quebec, QC,
G1R 1P8

FRANCE
*La Maison du Chocolat*
29 rue de Sèvres, 75006 Paris
*La Chocolatière*
4–6 rue de la Scellerie, 37000 Tours
*L'Artisan Chocolatier*

4 rue Camboulives, 81000 Albi

GERMANY
*Eilles Chocolatier*
Hauptwache 12, 60313 Frankfurt
*Leysieffer*
Kaufinger Tor (by Marienplatz),
80331 Munich

GREAT BRITAIN
*L'Artisan du Chocolat*
89, Lower Sloane Street,
London SW1W 8DA
*Bettys of Harrogate*
1 Parliament Street,
Harrogate HG1 2QU
*Charbonnel et Walker*
1 The Royal Arcade,
28 Old Bond Street,
London W1S 4BT
*Le Chocolatier*
8, Barrowmore Estate,
Great Barrow, Nr Chester
CH3 7JA
*Rococo*
321, King's Road,
London SW3 5EP
*Theobroma Cacao*
43, Turnham Green Terrace,
London W4 1RG
*Valvona and Crolla*
19 Elm Row,
Edinburgh EH7 4AA

IRELAND
*Butlers Irish Handmade Chocolates*
24 Wicklow Street,
Dublin 2

NETHERLANDS
*Salon du Chocolat*
Noordeinde 182, The Hague
2514GR

SWITZERLAND
*Chocolaterie Paul Stetter*
10 rue de Berne, 1202 Geneva
*Confiserie Baumann*
Balgritstrasse 2, 8008 Zurich

UNITED STATES
*Martine's*
6th Floor, Bloomingdale's,
1000 Third Avenue,
New York, NY 100221231
*The Truffle Shop*
408 Broad Street,
Nevada City, CA 95959
*Chocolate Connoisseur*
513 South Park Avenue,
Winter Park, FL 32789
*The Chocolate Truffle*
204 West Cummings Park,
Woburn, MA 01801
*Tom and Sally's Handmade Chocolates*
485 West River Road,
Brattleboro, VT 05302

# Museums

BELGIUM
*Musée du Cacao et du Chocolat*
Grand-Place 13,
1000 Brussels
*Musée du Chocolat Jacques*
Industriestrasse 16,
4700 Eupen

CANADA
*Erico Choco Museum*
634 rue Saint-Jean,
Faubourg Saint-Jean Baptiste,
QC Quebec, G1R 1P8
*Ganong Chocolate Museum*
73 Milltown Blvd,
St Stephen,
NB E3L 1G5

FRANCE
*Musée Art du Chocolat*
13 place Paul Saissac,
81310 Lisle sur Tarn
*Musée du Chocolat Henriet*
Place Clémenceau,
64200 Biarritz

GERMANY
*Imhoff Stollwerck*
Schokolademuseum
Reinauhafen 1a,
50678 Cologne

GREAT BRITAIN
*Cadbury World*
Linden Road,
Bournville,
Birmingham B30 2LD

ITALY
*Antica Norba Chocolate Museum*
Via Capo Dell' Acqua n°1,
04010 Norma (LT)

SPAIN
*Museu de la Xocolata*
Carrer Comerç 36,
08003 Barcelona

SWITZERLAND
*Chocolat Alprose SA*
Via Rompada 36,
6987 Caslano-Lugano

USA
*Hershey World*
170 West Hersheypark Drive,
Hershey, PA 17033
*Wilbur Chocolate Museum*
48 North Broad St, Lititz,
PA 17543

# Photographic credits

In addition to the photographs by Frédéric Vasseur, the rest of the documents reproduced in this book are from the author's collection, apart from:

p 6: photography courtesy of Green & Black's.
p 20 above, 52 above, 76 above, 91 below, 106 below, 115: photo CEDUS (Centre d'Étude et de Documentation du Sucre).
p 60 right and 61 left: photo Rowntree MacIntosh.
p 100: photo Chavanette.
p 116: photo Hotel Sacher, Vienna.

# Acknowledgements

The author is most grateful to Monsieur Christophe Chambeau-Fouquet, director general of the Chocolaterie Fouquet in Paris, for opening his factory to the photographer and thereby contributing so valuably to the book.

Many thanks to Cadbury Schweppes plc for their help with the English edition.

Editor: Colette Véron
Assisted by Brigitte Leblanc and Claire Cornubert

Designer: Sabine Büschenschütz

Layout: Ann Roumanille and Michel Cortey

Photogravure: Euresys, Baisieux

First published by Editions du Chêne, an imprint of Hachette-Livre
43 Quai de Grenelle, Paris 75905, Cedex 15, France
under the title *Le Chocolat*.
© 1998, Editions du Chêne-Hachette Livre
All rights reserved

English language translation produced by Translate-A-Book, Oxford

This edition published by Hachette Illustrated UK, Octopus Publishing Group,
2-4 Heron Quays, London, E14 4JP
English Translation © 2005, Octopus Publishing Group Ltd, London


ISBN 10: 1 84430 142 7
ISBN 13: 978 1 84430 142 3


Printed by Toppan Printing Co., (HK) Ltd.